FAITH IN DIVINE UNITY AND TRUST IN DIVINE PROVIDENCE

Kitāb al-Tawḥīd wa'l-Tawakkul

Book XXXV of

The Revival of the Religious Sciences

Iḥyā' ʿUlūm al-Dīn

AL-GHAZĀLĪ

FAITH IN DIVINE UNITY AND TRUST IN DIVINE PROVIDENCE

• *Kitāb al-Tawḥīd wa' l-Tawakkul* •

BOOK XXXV of THE REVIVAL OF THE RELIGIOIUS SCIENCES

Iḥyā' ʿUlūm al-Dīn • Translated with an INTRODUCTION and NOTES by DAVID B. BURRELL, C.S.C.

FONS VITAE

First published in 2001 by
Fons Vitae
49 Mockingbird Valley Drive
Louisville, KY 40207
email: fonsvitaeky@aol.com
website: www.fonsvitae.com

Library of Congress Control Number: 2001093410

ISBN 1-887752-35-8

Second printing, 2006
Third printing, 2013

Printed in Canada by Friesens
through Four Color Imports Ltd., Louisville, KY

CONTENTS

Abbreviations vii
Preface ix
Introduction xi
Notes to Introduction xxiii

FAITH IN DIVINE UNITY
AND TRUST IN DIVINE PROVIDENCE

Prologue: Explicating the Benefits of Trust in Divine Providence 3

THE FIRST PART
Explicating the Nature of Faith in Divine Unity [*tawḥīd*] as the Foundation of Trust in Divine Providence [*tawakkul*] 9

Notes to the First Part 47

THE SECOND PART
States of Trust in Divine Providence with Accompanying Practices 53

Chapter One: Explicating the State of Trust in Divine Providence 53

Chapter Two: Explanation of What [Sufi] Sheikhs Have Said about the States of Trust in Divine Providence 66

Chapter Three: Explanation of the Actions of Those Who Trust in Divine Providence 69

3.1. *On obtaining something beneficial which people lack* 69

CONTENTS, continued

3.11. *On obtaining what is beneficial for single persons* 70

3.12. *Explaining the trust in divine providence proper to heads of families* 88

3.13 *Using a parable to clarify the states of those who trust in God while depending on means* 97

3.2. *Attending to means by saving* 100

3.3. *On making use of means to repel injury and resist danger* 106

3.31. *Explanation of the conduct of those who trust in divine providence when their goods are stolen* 112

3.4. *On the effort to remove harm, as in treatment of disease and similar things* 118

3.41. *Explaining that dispensing with treatment belongs to some states and demonstrates the power of God, and how that does not contradict the practice of the messenger of God—may God's blessing and peace be upon him* 123

3.42. *Explanations countering those who say that foregoing treatment is more beneficial in every case* 132

3.43. *Explaining the states of those who trust in God with regard to disclosing or concealing illness* 137

Notes to the Second Part 140

APPENDIX: Persons Cited in Text 147

BIBLIOGRAPHY 162

ABBREVIATIONS

Abu Nu'aym	Abu Nu'aym al-Isfahānī, *Hilyāt al-Awliyā'*
EI2	*Encyclopaedia of Islam* (Second Edition)
Fihrist	Ibn al-Nadīm, *K. al-Fihrist*
GAS	Sezgin, *Geschichte...*
Ghāya	Ibn al-Jazarī, *Ghāyat al-nihāya...*
Hujwīrī	Nicholson (tr.), *Kashf al-maḥjūb*
Isāba	Ibn Hajar, *al-Isāba...*
Istī^{c}āb	Ibn ^{c}Abd al-Barr, *al-Istī^{c}āb...*
Kāshif	al-Dhahabī, *al-Kāshif...*
Mashāhīr	Ibn Hibbān, *Mashāhīr ^{c}ulamā' al-amsār...*
Qushayrī	Abū'l-Qāsim Qushayrī, *al-Risāla...*
Ṣafadī	al-Ṣafadī, *al-Wāfī bi' l-wafayāt*
SEI	*Shorter Encyclopaedia of Islam*
Siyar	al-Dhahabī, Muhammad b. Ahmad, *Siyar a^{c}lam al-nubalā'*
ST	Thomas Aquinas, *Summa Theologiae*
Sulamī	al-Sulamī, *Ṭabaqāt al-Ṣūfiyya*

PREFACE

This work has been some years in the making. After co-authoring a translation of the *Ninety-Nine Beautiful Names of God,* I was asked by Timothy Winter (then associated with the Islamic Texts Society in Cambridge) to translate this text, which he deemed to be the central theological treatise in Ghazālī's masterwork, *Iḥyā' ʿUlūm al-Dīn*. It was a real challenge, especially to complete without the beneficial offices of my Arabic teacher, Nazih Daher, with whom the initial translation had been undertaken. Yet others came to my assistance, notably Timothy Gianotti (now teaching at the Pennsylvania State University), who helped me utilize Arabic bibliographical sources to identify the Sufi sheikhs whose stories Ghazālī mines to illustrate authentic trust in God's providence. Timothy Winter's Appendix to his *Al-Ghazālī: The Remembrance of Death and the Afterlife* (Cambridge: Islamic Texts Society, 1989) also proved helpful here. In the final stage of preparation for publication, Farouk Ibrahim, of Cairo and my colleague for a semester at the Macdonald Centre for Muslim-Christian Relations at Hartford Seminary, read the entire text and saved me from many an egregious mistake. Those which remain are mine, of course, and every translator should welcome advice from readers who can improve what continually presents itself as a fascinating yet tedious task. For it is such readers who prove that it is not in the end thankless, even though one can never presume one's own version to be correct.

Qur'an translations have been adapted from Marmaduke Pickthall's *The Meaning of the Glorious Koran*, often supplemented by Kenneth Cragg's renderings in his *Readings in the Qur'an* (London: Collins, 1988), where he discusses the challenges in his introductory essay, "The Qur'an into English: A Translator's Apology." I am especially grateful to have been able to exploit Richard Gramlich's careful work of tracing hadiths in his German translation of this and related books from the *Iḥyā' ʿUlūm al-Dīn*, namely *Muhammed al-Gazzali's Lehre von den Stufen zur Gottesliebe: die Bücher 31-36* (Wiesbaden: Steiner, 1984). Qur'an references will be in italics, with chapter, verse [*sura:ayat*] following in brackets. Numbers in brackets in the text refer to pages in the edition of the *Iḥyā'* used; other material in brackets is added for explication or identification of key Arabic terms. My deepest gratitude is owed to Gray Henry for her intrepid work in matters Islamic and her keen oversight in publishing this translation. She had wisely entrusted the editing of the manuscript to Rob Baker, whose untimely death in Morocco stunned us all. I am especially grateful to Bernadette Dieker, who picked up that task with verve and a steady eye.

INTRODUCTION

The effect of this book of the *Iḥyā' ʿUlūm al-Dīn* [*Revivifying Religious Sciences*], together with *al-Iqtiṣād fi' l-iʿtiqād* [*Preserving the Faith*], is to qualify al-Ghazālī as a Muslim theologian in the full medieval meaning of that term, and not merely in the descriptive sense extended to include any thinker adept at *kalām*, or the dialectical defense of faith. That is, Ghazālī was intent on using human reason, as he found it elaborated in Ibn Sinā and others, not merely to defend the faith but to lead Muslim faithful to a deeper penetration of the mysteries of their revealed religion—the central mystery being the free creation of the universe by the one God.[1] The works of the philosophers themselves were not always helpful to him in their native state, so he had to set out first to purify them of their pretensions to offer an access to truth independent of and superior to that of divine revelation—the Qur'an. Hence his need to understand them thoroughly, embodied in the work entitled "The Intentions of the Philosophers [*Maqāsid al-falāsifā*]," itself conceived as an extended introduction (and hence also published as the *Muqāddima al-Tahāfut*) to his "Deconstruction of the Philosophers [*Tahāfut al-falāsifā*]."[2] The negative tone of this latter work, together with its detailed refutation by Averroës [Ibn Rushd: *Tahāfut al-Tahāfut*], has left the impression that Ghazālī should never be ranked with "the philosophers" but always left with "the theologians" as a defender of *kalām* orthodoxy in the face of reasonable inquiry. It is precisely that stereotype which this book challenges, and so can offer Ghazālī's own assistance to deconstruct the historical image which he helped to create for himself. It will involve challenging Averroës self-styled role as the pretended paragon of *philosophy*, and concentrate on Ghazālī's intent, leaving an assessment of his success to the reader.

The "Book of Faith in Divine Unity [*tawḥīd*] and Trust in Divine Providence [*tawakkul*]" is Book 35 in Ghazālī's masterwork, the *Iḥyā' ᶜUlūm al-Dīn*. The French summary of this *magnum opus*, "Révivification des sciences réligieuses," reminds us how forceful is the key term taken from the fourth form of the Arabic verb [*iḥyā*], probably best rendered in English as "Putting Life Back into Religious Learning."[3] For that would convey Ghazālī's intent, as well as his assessment of the state of such learning in his time. He is intent upon a clear understanding of matters religious, yet one which continues to give primacy to practice: faith is rooted in trust and must needs be expressed in a life of trust. The pretensions of the philosophers to understand the mysteries of *the heavens and the earth and all that is between them* [15:85], proceeding by conceptual argument alone, must be exposed as just that—pretension, in the face of the central assertion that the universe was *freely* created by the one sovereign God. Yet reason, which they are so intent to elaborate, will prove to be an indispensable tool in directing our minds and our hearts to understand how to think and how to live as a consequence of that signal truth.

Such is Ghazālī's intent. It is displayed in the structure of his *Iḥyā'* as well as in the pattern adopted for his treatise expounding the ninety-nine canonical "names" of God, where he devotes an extensive introduction to explaining the human practice of naming and how it might be understood in relation to the names which God has given Himself in the Qur'an.[4] It turns out that the only way to extend the limits of human knowledge of such divine things is by "adorning oneself" with the meaning of the names, so the commentary on each name begins with semantics and closes with a counsel: how one might oneself become more like God so presented. This pattern will become the master strategy of the *Iḥyā'* as well, where the entire gamut of Muslim life—beliefs together with practices—is laid out in a way which displays the importance of both *knowledge* and *state* [of being], that is, of understanding together with practice. Readers familiar with Aquinas will marvel at the way in which Ghazālī's master plan aligns with that thinker's insistence that theology is at once a speculative and a practical mode of knowing.[5]

It is fair to say that the *Kitab al-Tawḥīd wa' l-Tawakkul* plays an axial role among the other books in the *Iḥyā'*. For *tawḥīd*, or "faith in divine unity," sounds the distinctive note of Islam which grounds everything Muslims believe in the *shahāda*: "There is no god but God." Islamic reflection on *tawḥīd* is reminiscent of rabbinic commentary on divine unity as evidenced in the *shema*: "Hear, O Israel, the Lord our God, the Lord is One" (Deuteronomy 6:4). It is hardly at issue that God be one rather than many; it points instead directly to the injunction against idolatry: all Israelites know thereby that they must orient their entire lives to God—through the Torah, to be sure—and nowhere else. So a philosophical argument culminating in the assertion that God is one would hardly interest the rabbis, nor would it Ghazālī. Its conclusion may be true enough, but what is at issue is not the unity itself, but the implications of the community's *faith* in divine unity. Yet that cannot be a blind faith, so what is being asserted? That everything comes from God and that "there is no agent but God."

In cataloguing degrees of assent to this *shahāda*, Ghazālī notes: "The third kind [of believer] professes faith in divine unity in the sense that he sees but a single agent, since truth is revealed to him as it is in itself; and he only sees in reality a single agent, since reality has revealed itself to him as it is in itself because he has set his heart on determining to comprehend the word 'reality' [*haqīqa*]—and this stage belongs to lay folk as well as theologians" (11). He sketches out the two-part structure of the book by way of showing how *tawakkul*—trust in divine providence—is grounded in an articulate *tawḥīd*, as practice is anchored in faith, or *state* [of being] in *knowledge*. In doing so, he is even more insistent: this first part "will consist in showing you that there is no agent but God the Most High: of all that exists in creation—sustenance given or withheld, life or death, riches or poverty, and everything else that can be named, the sole one who initiated and originated it all is God Most High. And when this has been made clear to you, you will not see anything else, so that your fear will be of Him, your hope in Him, your trust in Him, and your security with Him, for He is the sole agent without any other. Everything else is in His service, for not even the smallest atom in the worlds of heaven and earth is independent of Him for its movement. If the gates of mystical insight were opened to you, this would be clear to you with a clarity more perfect than ordinary vision" (15-16).

These last words are telling, and signal Ghazālī's "method" in the first section elaborating faith in divine unity. There is no attempt to show *how* everything-that-is is of God; that would be beyond the capacity of our intellect to grasp. And should we try, we would invariably end up articulating something like Ibn Sinā's emanation scheme, modeled on logical inference and amounting to a twin denial of divine and of human freedom.[6] Indeed, when Ghazālī tries to articulate what he attributes to mystical insight, it sounds uncannily like Ibn Sinā, though he begins with a characteristic verse from the Qur'an: "*we did not create heaven and earth and what lies between them in jest; we did not create them but in truth* [44:38-39]. Now all that is between heaven and earth comes forth in a necessary order that is true and consequent, and it is inconceivable that it be otherwise than the way it comes forth, according to this order which exists.[7] For a consequent only follows because it awaits its condition; for a conditioned before a condition would be absurd, and absurdity cannot be ascribed to the being of an object of divine omnipotence. So knowledge [can be said to] follow upon sperm only if one supplies the condition of a living thing, and the will which comes after knowledge [can be said to] follow upon sperm only if the condition of knowledge be supplied as well. All of this offers a way of necessity and the order of truth. There is no room for play or chance in any of this; everything has its rationale and order. Understanding this is difficult..." (40). So he will offer images to move us away from a literal acceptance of the Avicenna-like scheme, for in such matters human reason can at best offer models; yet neither mode of apperception is privileged for Ghazālī, in contrast to "the philosophers," notably Averroës. The images offered by the Qur'an, however, will certainly take precedence.

But what about human freedom? Have we not exalted God's sovereign freedom, as the only agent there is, to the inevitable detriment of human initiative? It certainly appears that the intent of Ghazālī's images is to take us by the hand and lead us on, in hopes that we "may come to understand the emanation of things so ordained [*muqaddarāt*] from the eternal omnipotence, even though the omnipotent One is eternal and the things ordained [*maqdūrāt*] temporal. But this [train of thought] knocks on another door, to another world of the worlds of unveiling. So let us leave all that, since our aim is to offer counsel regarding the way to faith in divine unity in practice: that the true agent is One, that He is the subject of our fear and our hope, and the One in whom we trust and depend" (41-42). These gnomic words will be somewhat clarified in the text itself, but he also wants to show us that the test of our understanding of divine unity will not come by way of clever philosophical schemes but through a life of trust [*tawakkul*], in which concerted practice will bring each of us personally to the threshold of the only understanding possible here, that of "unveiling."[8] Yet some clarifications can be made; reason can offer some therapeutic hints to attenuate the apparent scandal.

He introduces a typically Muslim objection: "How can there be any common ground between faith in divine unity and the *sharīʿa* [religious law]? For the meaning of faith in divine unity is that there is no god but God Most High, and the meaning of the law lies in establishing the actions proper to human beings [as servants of God]. And if human beings are agents, how is it that God Most High is an agent?

Or if God Most High is an agent, how is a human being an agent? There is no way of understanding 'acting' as between these two agents. In response, I would say: indeed, there can be no understanding when there is but one meaning for 'agent.' But if it had two meanings, then the term comprehended could be attributed to each of them without contradiction, as when it is said that the emir killed someone, and also said that the executioner killed him; in one sense, the emir is the killer and in another sense, the executioner. Similarly, a human being is an agent in one sense, and God—Great and Glorious—is an agent in another. The sense in which God Most High is agent is that He is the originator[9] of existing things [*al-mukhtari' al-mawjūd*], while the sense in which a human being is an agent is that he is the locus [*maḥal*] in which power is created after will has been created, and that after knowledge had been created, so that power depends on will, and movement is linked to power, as a conditioned to its condition.[10] But depending on the power of God is like the dependence of effect on cause, and of the originated on the originator. So everything which depends on a power in such a way as it is the locus of the power is called 'agent' in a manner which expresses that fact of its dependence, much as the executioner can be called 'killer' and the emir a killer, since the killing depends on the power of both of them, yet in different respects. In that way both of them are called 'killer', and similarly, the things ordained [*maqrūrāt*] depend on two powers" (43).

He goes on to note how the Qur'an often attributes agency to God as well as to creatures, showing that revelation acknowledges and exploits the inherently analogous character of *agency* as exhibited in the multiple uses of the term 'agent'. This small clue offers us the best way of presenting Ghazālī's intent and his strategy to contemporary readers. What he wanted to do was to help believers to recognize that theirs is a unique perspective on the universe: each thing is related in its very existence to the one from whom it freely comes. (As Aquinas will put it: "the very existence of creatures is to-be-related to their creator"[*ST* 1.45.3].) Yet since we cannot articulate this founding and sustaining relationship conceptually, for to do so would trespass on divine freedom, we can only display our understanding by the way we live our life: trusting in the One who so sustains us.

To the recurring objection that all this amounts to *jabr*—coercion—on the part of God, he replies: "This has to do with the divine decree [*qadar*],[11] intimations of which we saw with respect to the faith in divine unity which brings about the state of trust in divine providence, and is only perfected by faith in the benevolence and wisdom [of God]. And if faith in divine unity brings about insight into the effects of causes, abundant faith in benevolence is what brings about confidence in the effects of the causes, and the state of trust in divine providence will only be perfected, as I shall relate, by confidence in the trustworthy One [*wakīl*] and tranquillity of heart towards the benevolent oversight of the [divine] sponsor. For this faith is indeed an exalted chapter in the chapters of faith, and the stories about it from the path of those experiencing the unveiling go on at length.... He enhanced knowledge, wisdom, and reason in a great number of [Sufi sheikhs], and then unveiled for them the effects of things [*al-ʿawāqil al-amūr*], apprising them of the secrets of the intelligible world, teaching them the subtleties of speech and the hidden springs of punishment, to the point where they were thus informed regarding what is good or evil, useful or harmful" (47-48).

This summary offers a springboard to part two of the book, which relates one Sufi story after another, while judiciously selecting them and weaving them into a pattern that allows persons to discriminate in making subtle decisions regarding the way they lead their lives aware of God's benevolent care, exhibiting the sorts of choices they make in typical situations. If Ghazālī closes the first part with what looks like a backward-looking conceptual reminder, he opens the way to an entirely different mode of consideration in part two: "Indeed, all this happens according to a necessary and true order, according to what is appropriate as it is appropriate, and in the measure proper to it; nor is anything more fitting, more perfect, and more attractive within the realm of possibility.[12] For if something were to exist and remind one of the sheer omnipotence [of God] and not of the good things accomplished by His action, that would utterly contradict [God's] generosity, and be an injustice contrary to the Just One.[13] And if God were not omnipotent, He would be impotent, thereby contradicting the nature of divinity" (48-49). Yet omnipotence cannot be the last word; generosity is a more operative one, for it modifies God's omnipotence in the direction of a benevolent creator. The upshot of *tawḥīd*, then, must be the believer's profound conviction "of the unalterable justice and excellence of things as they are ..., of the 'perfect rightness of the actual'."[14]

Eric Ormsby sees this conviction as the upshot of the ten years of seclusion and prayer following Ghazālī's spiritual crisis. By "the actual" he means what God has decreed, itself the product and reflection of divine wisdom. And by asserting the primacy of the actual over the possible, Ghazālī shows himself a true theologian. Contingency, for philosophers, tends to focus on the logical fact that "whatever exists could always be other than it is." Yet while it may be "logically correct and permissible to affirm that our world could be different than it is, ...it is not theologically correct and permissible—indeed, it is impious—to assert that our world could be better than it is. The world in all its circumstances remains unimpeachably right and just, and it is unsurpassably excellent."[15] Yet the excellence in question is not one which we can assess independently of the fact that it is the product of divine wisdom, so Ghazālī is not asserting that ours is the "best of all possible worlds," as though there were a set of such worlds "each of which might be ranked in terms of some intrinsic excellence." Such an assertion would quite miss the point of Ghazālī's quest: to find ways of expressing that relation of creator to creatures which quite resists formulation. The deconstructive moment had been his rejection of the emanation scheme; the constructive task is taken up in this twin discourse on faith in divine unity and trust in divine providence, but especially in this second part where practice will allow us to traverse domains which speculative reason cannot otherwise map.

What sort of a practice is *tawakkul*: trust in divine providence? It entails accepting whatever happens as part of the inscrutable decree of a just and merciful God. Yet such an action cannot be reduced to mere *resignation*, and so caricatured as "Islamic fatalism." It rather entails aligning oneself with things as they really are: in Ghazālī's terms, with the truth that there is no agent but God Most High. This requires effort since we cannot formulate the relationship between this single divine agent and the other agents which we know, and also because our ordinary perspective on things is not a true one: human society lives under the sign of *jāhiliyya* or pervasive ignorance. Yet this effort cannot be solely intellectual; that is, I cannot learn "the truth" in such a way as to align myself with it, in the time-honored fashion in which speculative reason is supposed to illuminate practical judgment. For the all-important relationship resists formulation. Nevertheless, by trying our best to act according to the conviction that the divine decree expresses the truth in events as they unfold, we can allow ourselves to be *shown* how things truly lie. So faith [*tawḥīd*] and practice [*tawakkul*] are reciprocal; neither is foundational. The understanding we can have is that of one journeying in faith, a *salīk*, the name which Sufis characteristically appropriated for themselves.

There are stages of trust in divine providence, to be sure, which Ghazālī catalogues as (1) the heart's relying on the trustworthy One [*wakīl*] alone, (2) a trust like that of a child in its mother, where the focus is less on the *trust* involved than on the person's orientation to the one in whom they trust; and (3) the notorious likeness of a corpse in the hands of its washers, where the relevant point is that such trust moves one quite beyond petition of any sort. Yet the operative factor is present already in the initial stage, which is not surpassed but only deepened by subsequent stages: trusting in the One alone. The formula for faith here is the hadith: "There is no might and power but in God," which Ghazālī shows to be equivalent to the Qur'anic *shahadah*: *There is no god but God*, thereby reminding us that the hadith does not enjoin us to trust in *power* or *might*, as attributes distinct from God, but in God alone. It is in this context that he selects stories of Sufi sheikhs, offering them as examples to help point us towards developing specific skills of trusting: habits of responding to different situations in such a way that one learns by acting how things are truly ordered, the truth of the decree. The principle operative throughout is that a policy of complete renunciation of means [*asbāb*] is contrary to divine wisdom, the *sunna Allah*, but those who journey in faith will be cognizant that there are different kinds of means, as they become aware of hidden as well as manifest ones.

The situations which he canvasses begin with the daily question of sustenance: should one seek it by working for it, or ought one wait for it to come to him or her? At issue here is a practice of some Sufis to sequester themselves in a mosque in prayer while relying on the generosity of the faithful, as well as more dramatic adventures of journeying into the desert without provisions. Ghazālī notes with approval that when the illustrious al-Hawwās undertook such journeys, he never left home without four items: a pot, a rope, scissors, and a needle and thread. For while he was convinced that God would provide for him on his journey, he realized that, according to the *sunna* of *Allah*, water would not be found on the surface of the desert (hence the pot and the rope), and should his sole tunic rip he would not be likely to run across a tailor (hence the scissors, needle and thread: "lest his nakedness be exposed"[76]). He also notes that judiciousness in such matters will differ considerably whether one be a single person or a householder. Other situations which involve a judicious practice of trust in divine providence include saving, repelling injury or resisting danger, our response to theft of our property, and the manner in which we relate to illness: ought one or may one simply dispense with all treatment? May we conceal the fact that we are ill from those who care for us, or must we disclose it? Here especially he strives for a sane "middle way": dispensing with treatment cannot be said always to be the "better way" for those who trust in God's providence.

The bevy of stories which Ghazālī mines offer living examples of the attitude proper to one who firmly believes in divine unity, namely, a total trust in God's providential care. He uses them to offer one object lesson after another of a way to take esoteric Sufi lore and allow it to inspire one's practice, as in the following: "Should you say that it has been said of certain ones that a lion put his paws on their shoulders without their being agitated, I would respond: It is said about certain ones that they ride lions and make them subservient, but there is no need to deceive yourselves about that station.[16] For even if it were authentic in itself, it would hardly be healthy to imitate a path which one learns about from someone else. That station is marked by an abundance of miracles and is certainly not a condition for trusting in God; it is rather replete with secrets which cannot be divined by those who have not attained it. You might also say: What are the signs by which I could know that I had attained it? I would respond: One who attains it does not need to look for signs. However, one of the signs of that station does in fact precede it: that a dog become subject to you, a dog which is always with you, indeed inside your skin, named Anger [or Resentment]. [Normally] it does not stop biting you and biting others. But if this dog becomes subservient to you, to the extent that when it becomes agitated and irritated it will be subject to you instantaneously, then your standing will be enhanced to the point where a lion, the very king of beasts, will be subject to you. It is more appropriate that the dog in your house be subject to you than a dog in the desert; but it is even more appropriate that the dog inside your skin be subject to you than the dog in your house. For if the dog within is not subject to you, how can you hope to make the dog outside subject to you" (115)?

So there is a school whereby we learn how to respond to what happens in such a way that we are shown how things are truly ordered. This school will involve learning from others who are more practiced in responding rightly; Ghazālī's judicious use of stories is intended to intimate the Sufi practice of master/disciple wherein the novice is helped to discern how to act. Philosophy is no longer identified as a higher wisdom; speculative reason is wholly subject to practical reason, but that is simply the inevitable implication of replacing the emanation scheme with an intentional creator![17] So the challenge of understanding the relation of the free creator to the universe becomes the task of rightly responding to events as they happen, in such a way that the true ordering of things, the divine decree, can be made manifest in one's actions-as-responses. Ghazālī expresses this relationship between speculative and practical reason by noting that we need to call upon both *knowledge* and *state* [of being] in guiding our actions according to a wholehearted trust in God. What he wishes to convey by those terms in tandem is an awareness of the very structure of the book itself: when put into practice, the *knowledge* which faith in divine unity brings can lead one to an habitual capacity to align one's otherwise errant responses to situation after situation according to that faith. In short, what Ghazālī terms a *state*, relying here on a Sufi anthropology, would be more familiar to western readers as Aristotle's stable "second nature" of virtue.

It is tied, however, not to the Hellenic paradigm of "the magnanimous man" but to a Quranic faith. This is also evident in his treatise on the names of God, for it is the ninety-nine names culled from the Qur'an, names by which God reveals the many "faces" of the divine, which offer a composite picture for human perfection. If we take names to identify attributes, then the book can be read in two distinct, yet related, ways: as a condensed summary of Islamic theology and as offering a revealed counterpart to Aristotle's *Ethics*. Perhaps enough has been said so far to begin to make my case for Ghazālī as an Islamic theologian, in the normative and not merely descriptive sense of that term. If he tends to resolve to mystical insight in places where philosophers would prefer conceptual schemes, one ought to acknowledge that he is also gesturing thereby that certain domains quite outstrip human conceptualizing. Yet more significant, however, is that everything he says about practice can be carried out quite independently of such "mystical insight," as indeed it must be for the vast majority of faithful.

Notes

1. See my *Freedom and Creation in Three Traditions* (Notre Dame IN: University of Notre Dame Press, 1993).

2. It is doubtless modish to translate '*tah¥fut*' as 'deconstruction', but then 'destruction' isn't quite right either; others have suggested 'stumbling'. The best English translation of this work of Ghaz¥lÏ's is by Michael Marmura: *Tah¥fut al-Fal¥sifa* (Provo UT: Brigham Young University, 2000). There is no current English (or western language) translation of the *Maq¥sid*, though one is proposed for the SUNY-Binghamton series under the general editorship of Parviz Morewedge. There are two Arabic versions, neither critical, one published by MuhÏ ad-DÏn SabrÏ al-KurdÏ, Cairo, 1331 A.H.; the other edited by Sulayman Duny¥ for Dar al-Ma'arif, Cairo, 1961.

3. G.-H. Bousquet (Analyse et Index) (Paris: Max Besson, 1955).

4. See Nazih Daher and my translation: *Al-Ghaz¥lÏ on the Ninety-Nine Beautiful Names of God* (Cambridge: Islamic Texts Society, 1992).

5. ST 1.1.4: "Sacred doctrine takes over both [speculative and practical] functions, in this being like the single knowledge whereby God knows himself and the things he makes" (cf. ST 1.14.5).

6. For a sketch of that model, see my *Knowing the Unknowable God* (Notre Dame IN: University of Notre Dame Press, 1986).

7. On the apparent connections with Ibn Sina here, see Richard M. Frank, *Creation and the Cosmic System: Al-Ghaz¥lÏ & Avicenna* (Heidelberg: Carl Winter, 1992).

8. This progression is reminiscent of his autobiographical sketch, the *Munqidh min al-dal¥l* (English translation by R. J. McCarthy, *Freedom and Fulfillment* [Boston: Twayne, 1980; Louisville: Fons Vitae, 2000]).

9. This term is not Quranic nor is it a name of God; cf. L,P. Fitzgerald, *Creation in al-TafsÏr al-KabÏr of Fakhr ad-Din al-R¥zÏ* (Ph.D. dissertation, Australian National University, 1992) 34.

10. Cf. Frank, *Creation and...*, 25.

11. William Chittick proposes that we render *qadar* as "the measuring out," and with respect to human understanding, the "mystery of the measuring out"—see *Faith and Practice in Islam* (Albany: State University of New York Press, 1992) 21, 189, 213.

12. This is Ghaz¥lÏ's celebrated claim regarding the universe—that is it "the best possible," a claim whose reception has been examined in detail by Eric Ormsby, *Theodicy in Islamic Thought* (Princeton NJ: Princeton University Press, 1984), and revisited in his contribution to *God and Creation*, edited by David Burrell and Bernard McGinn (Notre Dame IN: University of Notre Dame Press, 1990): "Creation in Time in Islamic Thought with Special Reference to al-Ghaz¥lÏ." See also Richard Frank, *Creation*... (note 7), 60-61.

13. *Al-¢Adl* [Just] is a name of God (cf. *99 Beautiful Names*, 92-96), and the following expression 'omnipotent' is derived from the name *al-Q¥dir* (*Ibid*., 131-32).

14. Ormsby, "Creation in Time ...," 256, quoting from his own *Theodicy*..., 32-91.

15. Ormsby, "Creation in Time...," 257.

16. Such stories are legion; see QushayrÏ, *Ris¥la* 166, 13-14; Ans¥rÏ, *Sharh ar-Ris¥la al-QushayrÏya* 4, 173.

17. See my "Why Not Pursue the Metaphor of Artisan and View God's Knowledge as Practical?" in Lenn E. Goodman, ed., *Neoplatonism and Jewish Thought* (Albany: State University of New York Press, 1992) 207-16.

THE BOOK OF FAITH IN DIVINE UNITY AND TRUST IN DIVINE PROVIDENCE

Kitāb al-Tawḥīd wa' l-Tawakkul

BOOK XXXV OF THE REVIVAL OF THE RELIGIOUS SCIENCES

Iḥyā' ʿUlūm al-Dīn

THE BOOK OF FAITH IN DIVINE UNITY AND TRUST IN DIVINE PROVIDENCE

Being the Fifth Book of the Fourth Set

of Colloquies comprising the *Iḥyā' ʿUlūm al-Dīn*

Prologue: Explicating the Benefits of Trust in Divine Providence

Praise be to God, ruler of visible and invisible worlds, distinguished by power and might, *upholder of the heavens with no need of support* [13:2], measuring out therefrom the sustenance of mankind. He is the master of hearts and breasts who diverts eyes from attending to means and causes to the cause of causes, raising their resolve from their inclination towards material things and ordinary concerns to the One who orders them all. As a result they worship none but the One whom they know to be the one, unique, eternal God, realizing that every species of creatures are servants like them [7:194]; so they do not seek their sustenance from them [29:17], but realize that there is no atom which does not owe its creation to God, nor animal which does not receive its sustenance from God [11:6]. So inasmuch as they realize that He sustains mankind continually and is the One who vouches for them, they will trust in Him and say: "*God is sufficient for us! Most excellent is He in Whom we trust* [*al-Wakīl*]" [3:173].

Blessed be Muhammad ﷺ who suppressed all idle talk, the guide to the straight path, and to his family, and may an abundance of peace be his.

To the point: Trust in God is one of the stages in the way of religion, and one of the stations of those who are certain in their convictions;[1] indeed it is one of the highest degrees of those who draw near [to God], so by its very nature it is hidden from knowledge yet impels one to action. It is difficult to comprehend how attending to causes and trusting in them amounts to idolatry in the face of faith in divine unity, yet paying no attention to them offends against the *sunna* and defames revelation. Yet to trust in causes without reflecting on the way in which they are causes diverts reason from its goal and leaves one immersed in a deluge of ignorance; whereas realizing the meaning of trust in God in a way which respects the exigencies of faith in divine unity, and of tradition and revelation as well, is freighted with obscurity and difficulties. Nor will one be able to remove this veil, given the intensity of the concealment at issue, without the mediation of scholars who adorn their eyes with the favor of God Most High by having recourse to the illumination of truth, so that they gain insight and confirmation, and then disseminate what they have seen insofar as they have examined it. We shall now begin by recounting the benefits of trust in God [*tawakkul*] by way of introduction; then follow that by a treatment of faith in divine unity [*tawḥīd*] in this half of the book, and speak about the state[2] of trust in God as well as its operation in the second half.

Explications of the Benefits of Trust in God

In the verses of the Qur'an, the Most High says: *So put your trust in God alone if you are indeed believers* [5:23], and the Great and Glorious says: *Let believers put their trust simply in God* [14:12], as the Most High says: *For whoever puts his trust in God, God will prove all sufficient* [65:3], and He also says —may He be praised and exalted— *God has love for those who put their trust in Him* [3:159]. Exalted is the station characterized by love of God Most High for His follower, where the sufficiency of God Most High secures all those close to Him. So it is that the one for whom God Most High suffices to give him all he needs, along with his love and wisdom, attains a singular success, for one who so loves will not be tormented, nor will he remain far from God or dissimulate. For the Most High says: *Is not God sufficient for his servant* [39:36]? So anyone who claims sufficiency from someone other than Him and refrains from trust in God denies this verse, and he will be asked on [260] the occasion of being interrogated by the Truth (as it is put by the Most High): *Has there come upon man any period of time in which he was a thing unremembered* [76:1]? The Great and Glorious also says: *Whoever trusts in God (will find that) lo! God is Mighty, Wise* [8:49]— that is to say: the mighty One does not humiliate those who seek refuge in Him, nor does He thwart those who long to be near Him or who have recourse to His security and protection. So the wise man will hardly fail, when he plans, to place trust in His planning. And the Most High says: *Those on whom you call apart from God are slaves like you* [7:194], thus explaining that everyone except God Most High is a subjected creature whose needs are like your needs, so how can you entrust yourself to them? As the Most High says: *Those you worship to the exclusion of God can afford you no sustenance at all. So seek sustenance from God, and give Him thanks* [29:17]. So the Great and Glorious: *God has the treasuries of the heavens and the earth; though the hypocrites have no idea of that* [63:7], and again: *He directs all things; there are none to intercede unless He has given leave* [10:3]. So everything mentioned in the Qur'an regarding the oneness of God [*tawḥīd*] is by way of counsel to divert attention from changing things and to fix our trust in the single Almighty One.

Now to the traditional reports [*ḥadith, aḥādith*].[3] The Prophet ﷺ said, as Ibn Masʿūd relates it, "I was shown the people in the hajj festival and I saw my people overflowing the mountains and the valleys and was astonished at their number and their array. When someone asked me 'Are you content?' I said, 'Indeed' and went on to say 'Here are seventy thousand entering paradise without having to make an accounting.' He said: 'Who are they, O Messenger of God?' To which he answered: 'Those who do not let themselves be branded nor seek omens nor engage in sorcery, but trust in their Lord.' Then ʿUkāsha [b. Mihsan al-Asadī] stood up and asked: 'O Messenger of God, pray to God that He may place me among them.' So the Messenger of God—may God's blessing and peace be upon him—said: 'O God, place him among them.' Then another rose and asked: 'O Messenger of God, pray to God that He may place me among them,' whereupon he said—may God's blessing and peace be upon him: 'ʿUkāsha came before you in this regard.'"[4] The Prophet ﷺ also said: "If you place your trust in God, truly trusting in Him, He will provide for you as He provides for the birds who are hungry in the morning yet satiated by evening."[5] He also said: "To those who devote themselves to God, Great and Glorious, God will satisfy them with every provision, providing for them in a manner beyond measure [cf. 65:3]; while for those who devote themselves to this world God will weary them with it."[6] And again, "Whoever takes pleasure in the fact that he is the richest of men is more secure with regard to what rests with God than what is in his own hands."[7] Moreover it is told of the Messenger of God—may God's blessings and peace be upon him—that when poverty befell his family, he said: "Rise up and pray, for that is what my Lord, Great and Glorious, commanded when He said: *Enjoin your people to worship and be constant therein* [20:132]."[8] He also said: "Those who have recourse to sorcery or cauterization have not placed their trust in God."[9]

[261] It is recounted how Gabriel asked Abraham—may peace be upon both of them—whether he needed anything, after he had been catapulted into the fire [by his pagan contemporaries, cf. 37:97]. He responded: "Not from you," true to His word: *God is all we need: He is the best trust we have* [3:173]—for that is what he said at the very moment he was taken to be catapulted. So it is that God Most High has revealed: *And Abraham was true to his word* [53:37]. God revealed to David—peace be upon him: "David, whoever takes refuge in Me and not in My creation, even though heaven and earth conspire against him, I will find him a way out."[10]

Continuing with the traditions, Said b. Jubayr said: "A scorpion bit me, and I swore to my mother not to have recourse to sorcerers, and my hand was restored to its original color as if it had never been bitten."[11] [Ibrahim] al-Hawwās recited the word of God the Most High—"Put your trust in the living One who dies not" (25:58)—to the end, and said: "After that verse, one has no need of taking refuge in anyone but God Most High."[12] It was said to one of the learned ones in his sleep: "Those who trust in God Most High protect their sustenance," and one of them said: "Do not be concerned about sustaining yourself with sustenance due to you from your work. Rather, let go of what is beyond you and only take from this world what God has prescribed for you." Yahyā b. Muᶜādh said: "In the very fact that one finds sustenance without looking for it is proof that sustenance is destined to find us." Ibrahim b. Adham said: "I asked a monk: 'Where do you get food to eat?' and he responded: 'That I do not know; ask my Lord whence He feeds me.'" Harim b. Hayyān said to Uways al-Qaranī:

"Where are you telling me to beg?" And pointing toward Syria, Harim asked: "How is it living there?" Uways answered: "Down with hearts like these! Doubt has so adulterated them that stern warning is of no use to them." Some have said: "When you are content with God as your trustee, you will find the way to all that is good." Let us ask God Most High for the beauty of a well-ordered life.

THE FIRST PART

Explicating the Nature of Faith in Divine Unity[*tawḥīd*] as the Foundation of Trust in God [*tawakkul*]

Know that trust in God pertains to faith, and all matters pertaining to faith may be classified by way of the knowledge, the state of being, and the activity proper to them. So trust in God can be classified according to knowledge as its source and activity as its fruit, while it is the state of being which renders the sense of the term '*tawakkul*'.

So let us begin to explain that knowledge which is the source, and which goes by the name of 'faith'. Yet faith involves judgment [*tasdīq*], and all judgment in the heart is knowledge, which is called 'certitude' [*yaqīn*] when it is firm. Many things pertain to certitude, however, and we only need those on which trust in God can be built. And that is faith in divine unity [*tawḥīd*], as His saying articulates it: *There is no God but Him* [37:35] alone, and *There is no sharer with Him* [6:163]; as well as faith in omnipotence which you articulate when you say: "Sovereignty is His," together with faith in generosity and wisdom which you indicate when you say *Praise be to Him* [64:1]. For whoever says: "There is no God but Him" alone, and "There is no sharer with Him," and *To Him belong sovereignty and praise, and He is the One Who Possesses Power* [*al-Qādir*] *over all things* [64:1]—to that one belongs the faith which is the root of trust in God. For the very force of this assertion induces a property indispensable to the heart which is mastered by it. Now faith in divine unity is the source and much could be said about it: it involves an understanding of revelation, yet some understandings of revelation depend upon practices undertaken in the midst of mystical states, and understanding of religious practices would not be complete without them. So we are only concerned with [faith in divine unity] to the extent that it pertains to practice, for otherwise the teaching of divine unity is a vast sea which is not easy to negotiate.

So let us explicate [262]: faith in divine unity has four stages, and may be divided into its core [3], its innermost core [4], its shell [2], and what contains its shell [1]. To accommodate weak understandings, let us liken this to a nut within its husk: for there are two shells and a core, and the innermost core contains oil. The first stage of faith in divine unity amounts to a person speaking the words "There is no god but God" while his heart is heedless or even denies it, as hypocrites may profess faith in divine unity. In the second stage one believes the meaning of the statement in his heart, as the community of Muslims believe it, and this is the faith of the common people. The third represents those who bear witness to [faith in divine unity] on the path of interior illumination by means of the light of truth, and that is the stage of those who are "drawing near," which takes place when one sees many things, but sees them emanating in their multiplicity from the Almighty One. The fourth stage is that of those who see only unity when they regard existence, which is the witness of righteous ones and those whom the Sufis call "annihilated" by faith in divine unity. For in the measure that they see only unity, they do not see themselves at all. And given that they do not regard themselves, taken up as they are into faith in divine unity, they have indeed been released from themselves to become totally absorbed in faith in this divine unity: that is, delivered from consideration of themselves and of creatures.

The first stage is linked to speech alone and protects the one who engages in it from the sword and the spear in this world. The second is connected with the meaning that one believes in his heart in comprehending what he says, given that his heart is free from deceit to the extent that his heart is taken up with [the meaning it asserts]. This stage is problematic for hearts which are not open and expanded, even though the mere avowal [of the *shahada*] serves to protects those who avow it from chastisement in the hereafter—given that they are convinced of it, and provided that the problems they may have with it are not compounded by the insubordination of sin. Yet one strategy is available to those who intend to attenuate and resolve the problems they have with it, and it is called heretical *innovation* [*bidᶜa*]; while another strategy exists for those who intend to reject such a ruse for resolving and attenuating these problems [with the *shahada*], but rather want to refine them so as to impress its [meaning] on the heart. This is called *theology* [*kalām*], while those who are proficient in it are called *theologians* [*mutakallim*]. These are opposed to innovators for their intent is to keep innovators from dissolving such problems in the hearts of the people, which singles out theologians as those professing faith in divine unity [*muwahhid*], insofar as they use their dialectical proficiency [*kalām*] to preserve the comprehension of the expression of faith in the divine unity in the hearts of the people rather than dissolve the problems [which the *shahada* may elicit]. The third stage represents those who profess faith in divine unity in the sense that they see only a single agent since truth is revealed to them as it is in itself; and they only see in reality a single agent since reality has revealed itself to them as it is in itself because they have set their heart on determining to comprehend the word 'reality' [*haqīqa*]—and this stage belongs to layfolk as well as theologians. For theologians are not distinguished from layfolk in the quality of their faith, but in the art by which they concoct arguments to prevent innovation from dissolving problems [connected with professing divine unity]. The fourth represents those who profess faith in divine unity in the sense that nothing other than unity is present to their sight, for they do not see anything insofar as it is many but only to the extent that it is one, and this is the farthest reach of faith in divine unity.

The first stage is like the husk of the nut, metaphorically speaking, while the second is like the inner shell, the third like the core, and the fourth like the oil emanating from the core. Now the husk of the nut, without the heart, is no good in itself: when eaten it is bitter to the taste, when seen from the inside it is disgusting to look at; if one tries to burn it, it smothers the fire and increases the smoke, and if it is left in the house it simply takes up space. So it is good for nothing except to be left for a while to preserve the heart, and then removed from it. In like manner, faith in divine unity confessed by the tongue alone without verification by the heart is of no advantage, does a great deal of harm, and is reprehensible when considered from the outside or from within. Nevertheless it is useful for a while to protect the inner shell up to the time of death. The inner shell is the heart and the body, and the profession of faith in divine unity of hypocrites protects their bodies from the sword of an armed incursion. For soldiers are not charged with penetrating the heart, since the sword can only reach the physical body, and that is the shell which will be removed from one at death, so whatever faith in divine unity may be associated with it is of no worth after death.

Now the inner shell is clearly advantageous in comparison with the husk, for it protects the oil, [that is, both the core and the innermost core], keeping it from spoiling when stored, and when it is separated it may be used as combustible material. However, its value is less than the oil, much as simple faith without any illumination is far more advantageous than mere utterance by the tongue, yet imperfect in value when compared with the illumination and revelation which is attained by those whose hearts have been purified and expanded by the light of truth arising within them. That expansion is the one meant by the word of God Most High: *And whomsoever it is God's will to guide, He expands his bosom to Islam* [6:125], and by the other saying of the Great and Glorious One: *Is he* [*the one*] *whose bosom God has expanded for Islam so that he follows a light from his Lord* [39:22]? Now the oil is priceless in one's soul, in comparison with the shell and all that it means. Nevertheless, it is not free from [263] adulterated products in comparison with the substance [the innermost core] extracted from it. Similarly, that faith in divine unity which is associated with practice is the highest goal of those on the way [to proximity with God], yet even this is not free from a sidelong glance towards other things, and of a penchant for the many—in comparison with those who see nothing but the one true reality [*al-ḥaqq*].

You might ask: How is it conceivable that one see nothing but unity when he sees the heavens and the earth and the other individual bodies, and they are countless? How can so many be one? You should know that this is the goal of the knowledge associated with mystical unveiling. It is not permitted to disseminate the secrets of this knowledge in a book, as those who know are wont to say: "Announcing the secret of divine sovereignty is infidelity [*kufr*];"[13] for it is quite distinct from the understanding associated with practices. Yet it is possible to find a way of forestalling your thinking it to be utterly farfetched. Consider the fact that things can be many under certain ways of looking at them or regarding them, but one under other ways of viewing or considering them: a man is many when one attends to his spirit, his body, his limbs, his blood vessels, his bones, and his inner organs; yet from another viewpoint and consideration—when we say of him that he is one man, he is one. He is one with respect to humanity. Yet how many individuals see a man without adverting to his manifold condition: his bowels, his blood vessels, his limbs, the intricacies of his spirit, his body and his inner organs?

The difference between these two [attitudes] lies in the way one is preoccupied, so as to attach little importance to one perspective or the other: those preoccupied with unity do not [apprehend] distinctions, and ever have the whole before their eyes, while those attending to multiplicity apprehend things in their distinctness. So it is with everything which exists, for creator and creatures alike, that there are many conflicting viewpoints and considerations, so that one consideration among many such is unity, while the considerations other than it are multiple, yet some of these are more manifold than others. The example of *man* hardly matches our intent here, yet it can alert us in general to the way in which multiplicity can result in a unified determination of viewpoints, so that this discussion might enable you to avoid denying or rejecting a station you have not attained, yet in which you can believe by a judgment of faith. For then you will have a share in it, in the measure that you are a believer by virtue of this faith in divine unity, even if what you believe is not a proper attribute of yours; just as when you believe in prophecy yet are not a prophet, you have a share in it by virtue of the strength of your faith.

The point of view which does not see anything but the one true reality can sometimes perdure, yet most often it occurs unexpectedly like a flash of lightning. It is quite unusual for it to perdure, however, as the story of al-Husayn b. Mansur al-Hallaj indicates, when he saw [Ibrahim] al-Hawwās setting out on a journey, and he asked him: "How are you?" He responded: "I am undertaking a journey to test my state of trust in God" (for he was among those who placed their trust in God), to which al-Hallaj remarked: "You are consuming your life with activity concerned with your inner self; what about letting yourself be consumed [*fanā*] by faith in divine unity?"[14] It is as though al-Hawwās was testing the third stage of faith in divine unity, while his student had attained the fourth stage. These stages of those seeking the oneness of God are offered as a kind of summary of faith in divine unity.

You might say: Certainly one can elucidate all this to the extent that one understands how trust in God is established. I would respond: So far as the fourth stage is concerned, discussion with a view to explaining it is not permitted, nor would trust in God be established on the basis of such a discussion; but a state of trust in God can be attained according to the third stage of faith in divine unity. The first stage is one of hypocrisy, and that is clear enough;

the second is one of simple faith [*iʿtiqād*] and can be found among the body of Muslims, while the method of confirming it by way of argument and resisting the allure of the innovators is presented in the science of *kalām*. (We have related a way of understanding that in the book *Al-iqtisād fi'l-iʿtiqād*.[15]) The third stage is the one on which trust in divine unity is established, and we would like to relate the manner in which trust in God depends on that faith, without spelling it out in a detail which would not be appropriate to a book like this.

Briefly, it will consist in showing you that there is no agent but God the Most High: of all that exists in creation—sustenance given or withheld, life or death, riches or poverty, and everything else that can be named—the sole one who initiated and originated it all is God Most High. And when this has been made clear to you, you will not see anything else, so that your fear will be of Him, your hope in Him, your trust in Him, and your security with Him, for He is the sole agent without any other. Everything else is in His service, for not even the smallest atom in the worlds of heaven and earth is independent of Him for its movement. If the gates of mystical insight were opened to you, this would be clear to you with a clarity more perfect than ordinary vision. But the devil can keep you at a certain stage in this [journey to] faith in divine unity, wishing to sow in your heart a suspicion of infidelity, and that in two ways. The first regards choice among living creatures [264]; the second concerns non-living things. Regarding the second, it is like your depending on rain for the seed to emerge, grow and flourish, on clouds for the rain to come down, on the cold for the clouds to converge, on the wind for the sailing vessel to stand erect and proceed on its course. But all this is infidelity [*kufr*] in the face of faith in divine unity, and ignorance [*jahl*] of the true reality of things, as the Most High says: *When they embark on the ships they pray to God, making their faith pure for Him alone, but when He brings them safely to land, behold! they ascribe partners* [*to Him*]

[29:65]. The sense of this verse is said to be that they were saying: "If the wind had not come up, we would not be saved," but whoever is given to understand the state of the world as it is in itself knows that the wind is part of the surrounding air, and that the air would not move itself were a mover not to move it, and another mover to move [that mover], and and so on until one arrives at the Prime Mover which has no mover nor it is moved in itself—the Great and Glorious.

The penchant of human beings to seek salvation from the wind could be likened to that of a person taken to be beheaded, yet when the king signed a decree annulling and dismissing the process, he began to concentrate on the ink, the paper, and the pen which were involved in the decree staying [his execution], saying: "Were it not for the pen, I would not have been released". It is as if he thought his salvation had come from the pen and not from the one moving the pen, yet this would be the height of ignorance. Whoever knows that the pen does not move by itself, but only moves as an instrument in the hand of a writer, does not consider the pen but directs his thanks to the writer alone. It could even be that the joy of being saved so overwhelmed him that he would thank the king and author [of the decree] without even adverting to the pen, the ink or the inkwell. Now the sun, moon, and stars, as well as rain, clouds and earth, along with all living and non-living things, are but instruments in the grasp of the divine decree [*qudra*], as a pen is subservient to the hand of an author. Moreover, this parable is offered to you not that you focus on the king who signed the decree as the author of the decree, for in truth it is God—may He be blessed and exalted—who is the author, according to the saying of the Most High: *You* [*Muhammad*] ﷺ *did not throw when you threw, but God threw* [8:17].[16] When it is revealed to you that everything in heaven and earth is subservient in this way, the devil will be repelled from you disappointed, and despair of adulterating your faith in divine unity with such infidelity.

This brings you to a second dangerous place, which is the consideration of free choice in the voluntary actions of living things . Many will say: How can you regard everything as coming from God, when a particular person gives you your sustenance by his own free choice, for if he so wills he gives it to you, and if he so wills he withdraws it from you? For it is this individual who beheads you with his sword, and so has power over you: if he so wills he beheads you and if he so wills, he desists. So how could you not fear him? How could you not put your hope in him, since your affairs are in his hands? You see this and have no doubt about it. But you could say to them in return: Indeed, if you consider the pen only insofar as it is an instrument, must you not also regard the one who writes with the pen, asking to whom he is subservient? Many stumble over this, but not those servants of God who have been liberated and over whom the devil has no power. For they see with the light of inner discernment that the author is subservient and compelled, just as all those with minimal [vision] can see how the pen is subservient. They realize that those with minimal vision err in this regard much as the ant would err were he to creep across the paper and see the tip of the pen blacken the paper. For his vision would not extend to the hand and its fingers, to say nothing of the one governing the hand, so he would err in thinking that the pen made what was white black, and all of this would be due to the shortness of his sight in regarding but the tip of the pen, due to the constriction of his pupils.

Similarly, those whose hearts are not illuminated by the light of God Most High bringing them to Islam (surrender on submission to God), will find their power of sight foreshortened from the vision of the Sovereign of heaven and earth, and from seeing how He is the One who dominates over all and sees all, and so keep them from the path to the author of it all. And that would be pure ignorance! But for those who possess their hearts and their vision, God Most High will make every atom in heaven and earth speak to them of His decree, which each thing articulates, to the point where they hear them celebrating and praising God Most High, and giving witness in their own way, despite their impotence of language, speaking without letters or sounds. Those *who are banished from the hearing* [26:212] do not hear them; and I do not mean an external hearing which fails to transcend sounds, for asses share in that, and what all beasts share is not important here. Rather I mean a kind of hearing which perceives words without letters or sounds, whether they be in Arabic or foreign tongues.

Yet you might say: But this is incredible and opposed to reason! Describe to me the manner of their speech: How it is they speak and of what they speak, how they praise and celebrate and give witness in their own way, despite their incapacity [for speech]? You should know that every atom in heaven and earth holds secret conversation with those who possess their hearts, and that it is without boundary or [265] limit. For these are words deriving from the sea of the word of God Most High, which has no limit: *Say* [*O Muhammad*]*: 'If the sea were nothing but ink for the words of my Lord, truly the sea would be run dry* [*before the words of my Lord were exhausted*]*'* [18:109]. Thus they exchange among themselves the secrets of this world and the intelligible world [*malakūt*]. To be sure, making this secret known is reprehensible; "The hearts of the pure are the graves of secrets."[17] Have you ever seen one faithful to a king's secrets and entrusted with keeping them secret announce that secret to a crowd of men? If it were permitted to make every secret known to us, would the Prophet ﷺ have said: "If you knew what I know, you would laugh very little and censure a great deal"?[18] [For if they knew], he would not have had to tell them [that they would censure and not laugh], nor would he have had to prohibit making known the secret of the divine decree,[19] or had to say: "If anyone talks of the stars, stop them; if they talk of the divine decrees, stop them; if they make reference to my companions, stop them."[20] Nor would he have had to entrust Hudayfa [b. al-Yamān] with some of his secrets.[21]

Now two obstacles stand in the way of giving an account of the secret conversations which the atoms of this world [*mulk*] and of the intelligible world [*malakūt*] hold with hearts possessed of vision.[22] The first is that it is impossible to communicate the secret; the second is that the words of these conversations exceed any boundary or limit. Yet we can offer a parable—the one we have already presented of the movement of the pen—and so in some small degree offer an account of their secret conversations by which one might understand in summary fashion how faith in divine unity is founded upon them. (We shall set out their words in letters and sounds as needed to understand them, even though they have neither letters nor sounds.) One of those observing from the vantage point of the niche of light of God Most High[23] said to the paper when he saw its surface blackened by the ink: "How is it that your surface was bright white and now black appears on it? Why did you blacken your surface? What is the cause [*sabab*] of it?" The paper said: "You are not being just to me in this dispute, for I did not blacken my surface by myself. Rather, ask the ink, for it was collected in the inkwell, which is a stable abode for it, and it went forth from its abode and came down upon my open surface wrongfully and maliciously." He said, "You are right," and asked the ink about it. The ink said: "You are not being just to me, for I was composed and calm in the inkwell, determined not to depart from it, when the pen encroached with malicious design, carried me away from my abode, removing me from my homeland, rent me asunder and spread me, as you can see, on the white surface. So ask him; not me." So he said, "You are right," and asked the pen about the cause of his malicious and evil action of removing the ink from its abode. The pen answered: "Ask the hand and fingers, for I was a reed growing free on the bank of the river in the midst of shrubs, and the hand came to me with a knife and cut away my husk, ripped my clothes off me, tore me away from my roots, and separated my tubes. Then they pared me and split my head, plunged me into the blackness of ink and its bitterness, and then enslaved me and made me walk on the tip of my head. So you have sprinkled salt in my wound with your question and your censure; let me go, and ask the one who subdued me." He said, "You are right," and asked the hand about his wrong and malice towards the pen in enslaving it.

The hand answered: "What am I but flesh and bone and blood? Have you ever seen flesh do wrong or a body move itself? I am but a mount subservient to the rider who rides me, who is called power [*qudra*] and might [*al-ʿizza*]. They are the ones who drive me and make me wander all over the earth. Don't you see that clods of earth, stones, and trees do not in any way leave their proper place nor do they move themselves unless they are ridden by the likes of this rider—some overpowering strength? Can you not see that the hands of a dead person are like me in shape and flesh, bone, and blood, yet there is no intercourse between them and a pen. Nor do I, taken by myself, have any intercourse with the pen. So ask the power how it is with me, for I am a mount roused by the one who rides me." He said, "You are right," and went on to ask the power what it had to do with employing the hand and especially about the way it enslaved it and drove it. The power said: "Stop blaming and censuring me! How many of those blamed are blameworthy, and how many of the blameworthy are without guilt? Moreover, are not my affairs hidden from you, so how can you think that I did wrong to the hand [266] in riding it? For I was on it as a rider before any movement, but I did not make it move nor did I reduce it to slavery. On the other hand, I was sleeping so peacefully that one might think that I was dead or absent, for I was neither in motion nor moving anything until the one charged with inciting and compelling me came to me and I was brought to the state in which you see me. For while I possess the power of assisting him, I have no power to resist him; the one so commissioned is called *will* [*irāda*]. I only know him by his name, his sudden attack, and his tyrannical rule, for he awakens me from the depths of sleep and compels me to what would otherwise be quite different, were it open to me or had I any opinion on the matter."[24]

[Our inquirer, let us call him 'the pilgrim'] said, "You are right," and then he asked the will: "What made you run after this power in peaceful repose so as to put it in motion and overpower it in such a way that it cannot find escape or repose?" The will responded: "Don't be so hasty to accuse me, for I may be excused from your rebuke. For I do not incite myself but am incited; I do not bring myself to life, but am called forth by an overpowering judgment and a peremptory command. Before it came I was in repose, but a messenger of knowledge came to me from the anteroom of the heart with an utterance of reason to dispatch to the power, and I dispatched it under duress. For I am poor and subservient beneath the compulsion of knowledge and of reason. Nor am I conscious of any offence in depending on the judgment and command, in serving it, or in being compelled to obey it. I am rather conscious of being in repose and resting until this child of the conquering one comes to me, and I become utterly dependent upon this judgment—just or unjust—and quite compelled to obey it. Whenever his judgment has determined something I have no power left to oppose it. By my life! So long as he keeps to himself or his judgment is vacillating, I am in repose, but otherwise I am quite aware of his judgment and awaiting it. Yet when his judgment is decided, I am troubled in disposition and compelled to obey it, and I dispatch the power to carry out his judgment as it is presents itself. So ask the intellect how it is with me, and stop censuring me, for with me it is like the poet said:

When you leave people, they are the ones who are strong,
But when you do not separate from them, they are the ones who will leave.

The pilgrim said, "You are right," and he approached knowledge, reason, and the heart, seeking them out and censuring them for arousing the will, and reducing it to bondage to dispatch the power. Reason said: "I am a light which does not light itself but is lit;" while the heart said: "I am a slate which does not extend itself but is extended;" and knowledge said: "As for me, I am an engraving inscribed on the blank slate of the heart to be illuminated by the light of reason, but I do not inscribe myself. How often has this slate been free of me! Ask the pen about me, for the inscription cannot be without the pen." With this, the questioner began to stammer, for the answer did not convince him. He said: "How long have I toiled on this path, and [traversed] many stations, yet each one from whom I wanted to gain some inner knowledge [*maʿrifa*] of these matters directed me from him to another. Nevertheless, it was better for me to hear many things repeated, even though I heard contradictory statements, which I did not take to heart, and excuses clearly intended to put off the question. But as for your saying: "I am an inscription and a design, and a pen drew me"—that I do not understand. For I only know pens made of reeds and slates made of iron or wood, inscriptions in ink and lights with flames, yet I have heard in this station news of slates, lights, inscriptions, and pens, and I cannot attest to things of that sort. I heard a grinding noise but I do not see any meal."

The pen said to him: "You are right in what you say, yet your provisions are few and your supplies scanty [for the journey], so your progress will be minimal. You should know that you will face many dangers on the path, so the right thing for you would be to give up [the search] and cease what you are doing. This is not your nest, so leave it;

yet everything is easy for those who are fashioned for it. But if you really want to follow the path to its goal, what you will hear and see will be brilliant. You should know that there are three worlds on your path. The earthly world [*mulk*] of visible things is the first, containing paper, ink, pens, and hands; and you will easily pass beyond this station. The second world is the intelligible world [*malakūt*], and that lies beyond me. If you pass beyond me you will reach its station, and there lie wide deserts, towering mountains, and teeming seas; and I do not know how you will fare there. The third is the world of compulsion [*jabarūt*], which lies between the earthly world and the intelligible world. You have already traversed three of their stations in the foremost stations of power, will, and knowledge."

"This world is midway between the earthly and visible world and the intelligible world, in that the way is easier to negotiate in the earthly world while the intelligible world is more difficult to traverse. Standing between the earthly and intelligible worlds, the world of compulsion can be likened to a ship which is in motion: as between being in the water or on earth, it is not as turbulent as being in the water yet not as secure as being on land. Whoever walks on [267] the earth walks in the earthly and visible world but if one can surpass one's own power to the point of being able to sail in a ship, that will be like moving in the world of compulsion. So anyone who comes to the point of traversing water without a ship moves in the intelligible world without any anxiety. But if you are unable to walk on water, better to stop there. For you have already gone beyond the land and left the ship behind, so nothing remains under your feet [lit., between your hands] but water. The intelligible world begins with a vision of the pen by which knowledge writes on the slate of the heart, and ends with that certainty [*yaqīn*] by which one walks on water, as you have heard in the saying of the Messenger of God ﷺ about Jesus—peace be upon him—in response to the story that he walked on water: 'were his certainty even greater, he would have walked on air'."[25]

At this point the pilgrim asked: "I am confused regarding these matters and my heart has been incited to fear from the way you have described what lies along the path, so I do not know whether or not I will be able to traverse the wasteland which you describe. Are there any signs to address those fears?" Knowledge responded: "Indeed; open your inner vision and concentrate the light [*ḍau'*] of your eyes and fix your gaze in my direction. If the pen appears to you with which I write on the slate of the heart, then it is likely that you are fit for this path. If you have gone beyond everything in the world of power, and are standing knocking at the door of the intelligible world, the pen will be revealed. Will you not see what the Prophet ﷺ in the beginning of his mission [saw] in the unveiling of the pen, when it revealed to him: *Recite: Your Lord is the most Generous, who teaches by the pen, teaching man what he knows not* [96:3-5]?" The pilgrim said: "My inner vision is opened, and I am fixing my eyes on it. But by God, I do not see reed or wood, and I only know pens like that." But knowledge responded: "You have already left benefits behind, and have you ever heard that the furniture of the house can be compared to the lord of the house? Do you not know that God Most High is not, in His essence, like any other essence? Similarly, His hand is not like other hands, nor His pen like other pens, nor His word like other words, nor His writing like other writing. These divine matters belong to the intelligible world: God the Most High in His essence is neither bodily nor in a place—by contrast with all that is not He."

"His hand, unlike other hands, is not composed of flesh, blood, and bone, nor is His pen made from a reed, nor His slate of wood, nor His word of sounds and syllables, nor His writing of ciphers and letters, nor His ink of vitriol and oak apples. And if you do not see these things in this way, I can only regard you as ambivalent [lit: bisexual] as between the 'masculinity' of the proponents of *tanzīh* ['negative theology', who remove all attributes from divinity] and the 'femininity' of the proponents of *tashbīh* ['anthropomorphism', who insist on granting God all Qur'anic attributes], oscillating between this one and that one, belonging neither to one party nor the other.[26] How can you keep the divine essence free from bodily attributes, and God's word from the connotation of syllables and sounds, if initially you hesitate regarding His hand, His pen, His slate, and His writing? If you understand the words of the Prophet ﷺ, 'God created Adam according to His form'[27] as though the form were exterior and perceptible by sight, that would be pure anthropomorphism—as it is said: 'Be a wholehearted Jew, and if not, don't play games with the Torah.'[28] But if you understand the hadith to refer to an inner form perceptible by inner vision, and not by ordinary sight, that is utterly unadulterated and 'masculine' holiness, and aligned with the path: *You are in the holy valley of Tuwā,' so 'hearken (in the secret place of your heart) to what is inspired* [20:12, 13]. You may find *guidance at the fire* [20:10] or perhaps, along with those charged with the accoutrements of the throne; it will be announced to you as it was to Moses عليه السلام : *I am your Lord* [20:12]."

When the pilgrim heard this from knowledge, he was conscious of his own deficiency, and that he was ambivalent as between *tashbīh* ["anthropomorphism"] and *tanzīh* ["negative theology"]. His heart was inflamed with a vehement anger at his own soul [*nafs*] when he regarded it with an eye to its shortcomings. But there was his oil in the niche of his heart, which *began to glow though no fire touched it* [24:35], so that what knowledge had presented to him, coupled with his own anger, ignited his oil so that it reached a point where it was *light upon light* [24:35]. So knowledge said to him: "Seize this opportunity to open your eyes and perhaps you will find 'guidance at the fire' (20:10]." So he opened his eyes and the heavenly pen was unveiled to him, and it was as knowledge had described it according to *tanzīh*: neither of wood nor a reed, neither with a point nor an end, and it was writing uninterruptedly on the hearts of human beings every kind of knowledge—as though there were a tip in every heart even though it had no tip. He was utterly astonished and said: "How good a companion knowledge is! May God reward him with all good things on my behalf! For it has now become clear to me how right are the things he said about the attributes of the pen; I see it is a pen unlike other pens." At this point he took leave of knowledge, thanking him, saying, "I have been with you for some time, speaking with you, and I am determined to continue journeying until I meet the pen and ask it about itself."

So he returned to the pen and asked him: "Why is it that you, O pen, write continually on hearts with a knowledge by which you incite wills to activate the power and direct it to its objects?" The pen responded: "Have you already forgotten what you saw in the world of earthly and visible things, and heard the pen answer when you asked it about what it then passed [268] on to you about the hand?" The pilgrim answered: "I have not forgotten that." The pen responded: "My answer is similar to his." "But then how is it that you are not like him?" The pen said: "Did you not hear [the hadith] that God the Most High created Adam according to His form?" "Yes." "Then ask the man who is called 'the king's right hand' how it is with me, for I am in his grip. He is the one who wields me and I am pressed into serving him. There is no difference between the divine and human pens with regard to their subjugation; they are only different in outward form." "But who is the 'right hand of the king'?" the pilgrim asked. "Have you not heard the saying of the Most High," asked the pen: *the heavens are rolled up in His right hand* [39:67]?" "Indeed." He said: "Pens are in the grip of His right hand as well; He is the One who wields them."

The pilgrim continued on from there to the "right hand" where he saw it and regarded its marvels, even greater than the marvels of the pen. He was not able to describe or explain any of them; indeed, many volumes could not even include one hundredth of its description. In sum, however, [one can say that] it is not like other right hands, as the hand is not like other hands, nor the fingers like other fingers. As he saw the pen moving in His grip and so realized who was responsible for the pen, he asked the right hand about its role as the one who sets the pen in motion. He responded: "My answer will be like the one you heard from the right hand which you saw in the visible world. It is a screen for the power; since the hand has no authority in itself, there can be no doubt that the power moves it." The pilgrim journeyed on to the world of power [*ʿālam al-qudrah*] and saw there wonders which made him disdain those he had seen before, and when he asked regarding the movement of the right hand, he was told: "I am only an attribute; ask the One who possesses power [*al-Qādir*], for authority belongs to the one possessing the attribute rather than to the attribute itself." At this point he was about to turn away and forsake any further questioning, when he was held fast by *the surely grounded word* [14:27] proclaimed from behind the veil of the pavilions of the divine presence: *He is not to be questioned as to what He does; it is they who are to be questioned* [21:23]. Dread of the divine presence enveloped him and he fell thunderstruck, shaken by the fact of being so overwhelmed.

When he recovered, he said: "Glory be to You! How exalted is Your estate! I am perishing before you; I put all my trust in You, I believe You to be King, Unique, Compelling, Dominator.[29] I am not afraid of anything other than You, nor do I return to anyone other than You. I seek refuge from Your punishment in Your forgiveness alone, and from Your disapproval in Your approval. What can I do but beseech You, humbling myself before You, and pray humbly in Your hand? So I say: '*Open my heart* [20:25] that I may know You, and loosen my tongue that I may praise you.'" Then it was announced to him from behind the veil:

"Take care not to aspire to praise greater than the lord of the Prophets. Rather turn to him, take what he gives you and renounce what he forbids you, saying what he says to you. For there is nothing more [to be said] at this level than his saying: 'Praise be to you! I do not know how to praise You; You are as You praise Yourself'."[30] To which the pilgrim said: "My God! If the tongue is unable to praise You, how can the heart aspire to know You?" Then it was announced: "Take care not to stand out over the necks of the righteous ones.[31] Rather turn to the great and righteous one [Abū-Bakr] and emulate him, for the companions of the lord of the Prophets 'are like one of the stars: follow them and you will be rightly guided'.[32] Have you not heard what he said: 'The very inability to attain knowledge is itself knowledge'.[33] It is enough for you to share in Our presence to know that you are excluded from Our presence, incapable of glancing at Our beauty and Our glory."

This servant, the pilgrim, returned and apologized for his questions and his censures, saying to the right hand, the pen, knowledge, will, power, and the rest: "Accept my apologies, for I am a stranger only recently arrived in this land, and anyone who comes here is perplexed. I was resisting only because of my limitations and my ignorance. Now it is only right for me to apologize to you as it has been unveiled to me that the One who alone [possesses] the earthly world, the intelligible world, majesty and power, is the One, the Dominator.[34] And all of you are in His service, under His domination and His power, continually in His grasp—He is *the First and the Last, the Manifest and the Hidden* [57:3]."[35] If anyone repeats that in the visible world people will consider it far-fetched and say to him: "How can something be first and last, for these two attributes are opposed to one another? For what is first is not last, and what is manifest is not hidden." To which he will respond: He is first with respect to existing things, for they all emanate from Him one after another in an ordered fashion; and He is last with respect to initiating undertakings, for they will only continue to progress from one stage to another in such a way as to arrive at their goal in His presence. So He is the last point on [their] journey, which makes Him the last in the visible world and the first in existence. In a similar fashion, He is hidden from those taken up with the visible world, seeking to perceive Him with their five senses, yet manifest to those who seek Him by the light which kindles in their hearts [269], by an inner vision which offers a hidden opening to the intelligible world. This is what faith in divine unity consists in for those actively journeying on the path of such faith; that is, those to whom it has been unveiled that there is but one agent.

Now you might well say: So it turns out that such a faith in divine unity is grounded in faith in the intelligible world, so what could be the way for someone who either does not understand that world or even denies it? To which I would say: There is no cure for one who denies [such a world] other than to say to him: Your denying the intelligible world is like the Buddhists' denying the world of power [*jabarūt*]. For they restrict knowledge to the five senses, thereby denying power, will, and knowledge, since we cannot perceive them by the five senses, while those characteristics specific to the visible world are linked necessarily to the five senses. To which he would respond: Then count me among them, for all I can discover through the five senses is the visible world, and I do not know anything else. One could then say: Your denying what we see beyond the five senses is like the sophists' denial of the five senses, when they say: We do not trust what we see; perhaps we are seeing in a dream. To which one can respond: I am like the rest of men, and I err now and again in [perceiving] sensible objects. So it must be said that this is someone whose state of health is corrupt and for whom a cure is impossible, but there are very few of those. Moreover, every sick person does not lie beyond the cure of doctors, even though this be the case with one who denies [the intelligible world].

With regard to those who do not deny it but rather fail to understand, the way of pilgrims will be relevant to them if they but direct their attention to the eye by which one sees the intelligible world. If they find it sound at root, even though impure liquid may have fallen into it, they will set about to remove [that substance] and devote themselves to cleansing it, as eye doctors occupy themselves with eyes which see visible things. When one's sight has been set aright, it will lead to the way of the pilgrims, just as the Prophet ﷺ did with his chosen companions. But for those who cannot accept a cure, it will be impossible for them to pursue the path to faith in divine unity which we have described for them, since they will not be able to overhear the discussion between the atoms of the visible world and of the intelligible world as it witnesses to faith in divine unity. They will speak to such people in syllables and sounds, so bringing the summit of faith in divine unity to the plane of their comprehension. And there is a kind of belief in unity in the visible world, for everyone knows that a house is spoiled by two owners, or a land by two rulers, and one's reason says accordingly: the God of the world is one, and the ruler is one.[36] So it is said: *If there were gods beside God,* [*both heaven and earth*] *would be disordered* [21:22]. All this belongs to the "taste" [*dhawq*] which accompanies what one sees in the visible world, in such a way that the conviction of faith in divine unity is implanted in one's heart by this path adapted to one's reason. That is why He sent the Qur'an down in the very Arabic tongue in which they were accustomed to converse.

You may ask: Is something like this conviction concerning faith in divine unity suitable as a foundation for trust in divine providence? To which I would respond, yes; for when the conviction is strong it will do the work of unveiling, given even a trace of the mystical states. But given that [the conviction] is weak in most cases, it is more usual that it quickly ushers in confusion and stumbling. So one who possesses this conviction needs a theologian [*mutakallim*] to protect it with dialectical argumentation [*kalām*]. Or one must learn to use theology oneself, to protect the conviction which he has received from his teachers or his parents or his countrymen. As for those who spy the way and follow it on their own, [they should know that] even were the covering to be unveiled, that alone will not effectively add up to certainty [*yaqīn*]. For should [their perception] lead to clarity, it would still be like one who saw a man in the evening light [lit.: time of travelling]: he would not gain the certainty that it was a man merely by the rising of the sun, but only by clarifying the details of His creation.

One may liken people of the unveiling with people of conviction as one might compare the sorcerers of pharaoh with the associates of the Samiri.[37] For the sorcerers of pharaoh were familiar with the range of action of sorcerers, having observed and practiced it for a long time. So when they saw Moses—peace be upon him—breach the boundaries of sorcery and unveil to them the way matters truly lie, they did not heed the warning of pharaoh: "*I will cut off your hands and feet on alternate sides*" [20:71], but they replied: "*We will never set more store by you than by the clear evidences that have come to us and the One who fashioned us. Decree what you decree: you will only be arbiter concerning the life of this present world*" [20:72]. So it is that proof and unveiling proscribe vacillation. Associates of Samiri, on the other hand, had put their faith in gazing upon the serpent, but when they looked on the calf of Samiri and heard its lowing, they changed and listened to his words: "*This is your god, the erstwhile god of Moses [whom he has forgotten]*" [20:88], overlooking the fact that *it made no response to them, that it had no power at all* [270] *to hurt or profit* [20:89]. Now those who put their faith in gazing on a serpent will undoubtedly prove unfaithful when they look on a calf, because both belong to the visible world, where there are many oppositions and contradictions; whereas the intelligible world belongs to God the Most High and so cannot sustain any oppositions or contradictions at all.

You might say: What you have said about faith in divine unity is clear with regard to subservient means and causes; all of that is clear except for the movements of human beings, for they initiate movement as they will or remain at rest as they will, so how can they be subservient? But you should know that if things were the way you say, one would will [*yushā*] when one intended [*arāda*] to will, and would not will if one did not intend to will; but this does not provide a firm footing and falls into error. For we know that people will whether they intend to will or not, for willing is not up to them. And if it were to belong to one [to will], then another [willing] would be required to will, and so on *ad infinitum*. Yet while it does not belong to a person to will, nevertheless it is the activity of willing, as it directs the power to its actions, which moves the power to act. But one need not derive a contradiction from that fact, since the motion follows necessarily from the power and the power moves necessarily.[38] The decisiveness of willing comes from this fact, for willing takes place in the heart necessarily. Yet it is an orderly necessity by which some things occur after others. It does not belong to humans to stand in the way of the emergence [*wujūd*] of willing, nor the connection of the power with its action, nor the emergence of motion after the will has aroused the power, for all this happens of necessity.

Now you may say: This is sheer constraint [*jabr*] and constraint is in direct opposition to freedom of choice [*ikhtiyār*]. And you do not deny freedom of choice, so how can those who are constrained also freely choose? To which I would respond: if the covering were unveiled, you would recognize that there is constraint in the course of freedom of choice, in such a way that it is itself constrained to choose. But how can you comprehend this when you do not understand freedom of choice? So let us explain freedom of choice in the language of the theologians, but in a concise manner so as neither to intrude nor inconvenience, since the aim of this book is only the understanding of religious practice. I can say that the language of action is applied to human beings in three ways. So we say that a person writes with his fingers and breathes with his lungs, and that one's neck displaces water when his body comes into relation with it, so that displacing water is attributed to him, just as breathing and writing is. Yet these three are one in the essential reality of necessity and constraint, although they differ in ways other than that, which I shall clarify for you from three vantage points.

Insofar as it happens to him, we call his displacing water a natural action, while we call his breathing a voluntary action [*irādīan*], and his writing a freely chosen action [*ikhtiyārīan*]. Natural action gives evidence of constraint to the extent that something happens to the surface of the water so that it overflows into the air, inevitably displacing the air, so that displacing necessarily follows upon overflowing. It is similar with breathing, for the movement of the throat is related to wanting to breathe as displacing of water is related to the weight of the body; since where there is weight there is displacement in the wake of it, so where there is no willing there is no breathing. In a similar way, if one aims a pin at a person's eye, he will close his eyelids of necessity, and were he to want to hold them open he could not, even though this necessary shutting of the eyelids is an intentional action. Moreover, if the point of a pin were presented to one's perception, this necessary wanting to close [one's eyelids] would occur along with the movement; and were one to want to resist that, he would not be able to, even though it is an action of the power and the will. So the fact that this [voluntary] action is connected with natural action also makes it necessary.

The third form of action, that of free choice, is an ambiguous notion like writing and speaking. For it is said of free choice that one wills to do it or one wills not to do it, or sometimes that one does not will; thereby imagining that one knows how matters lie, but in fact only manifesting one's ignorance of the meaning of freedom of choice. So let us remove the veil from it to explain it. Freedom of choice follows upon the knowledge that judges whether a thing is appropriate for you, for things are divided into what your outer or inner perception judges, without confusion or uncertainty, to be right for you, notably regarding those things about which reason has hitherto been indecisive. For you determine without hesitation [what to do] when someone, for example, aims a pin at your eye or a sword at your body, nor have you any uncertainty realizing that you should repel them for your own good and benefit. And it is hardly wrong for the will to be aroused by reason or the power by the will, or for the eyelids to be put into motion by a thrust, or the hand moved by a sword thrust—yet without any deliberation or reflection. So it is with the will. [That is, there is a dimension of necessity at the very heart of freedom of choice].

There are things, however, about which discrimination and reason remain undecided, without being able to discern whether they are appropriate or not, so that one needs to deliberate and reflect whether it is better to do them or to let them pass. [271] When after reflection and deliberation reason decides upon one of these courses of action, it prefers connecting that with what it determined without reflection or deliberation. At this point the will is aroused just as it is aroused by the thrust of a sword or the tip of a spear. So we call this will [*irāda*] which is aroused to action by what appears good to reason "freedom of choice" [*ikhtiyār*], as it craves the good [*al-khaīr*]. By that I mean that it is [necessarily] aroused by what appears to reason to be good for it, which is the very source of this willing. Nor does this willing need to wait to be aroused by what it is expecting, for it is an evident good with respect to action, differing from the evident good in [resisting] the thrust of the sword only in that this took place spontaneously without any reflection while the other required reflection.

So freedom of choice consists in a specific willing which is aroused by a counsel of reason which also, once perceived, brings it to its term. It is said about this [process] that reason is required for it to distinguish which is the better of two goods or the lesser of two evils. We cannot conceive the will being aroused except by movement of the senses or the imagination, or by a decisive movement on the part of reason. As a result, if someone wanted, for example, to slit his own throat, he would not be able to do so—not for want of power in his hand nor for lack of a knife, but because the personal will to motivate the power is not present.[39] And the will is not present because it is not aroused by the movement of reason or the evident advantage of doing the appropriate action. Indeed, since killing himself is not an action appropriate for him, he remains unable to do it—despite the strength in his arms to kill himself—without bringing on a reaction so distressing that he could not bear it. In this case, reason withholds judgment and hesitates, because it is in doubt regarding which of the two evils is worse, yet if after reflection it thinks it better to refrain from killing, as the lesser evil, then it is not possible for him to kill himself. Yet if he should judge that killing is the lesser evil, and if his judgment is decisive—no longer simply inclining towards it nor turning away from it—then the will and the power will be aroused and he will destroy himself.

Such a person would then be like someone whom one was pursuing with a sword to kill him. Supposing that he threw himself from a roof and so met his end, [that action itself] would not have occured to him nor would he have been able not to throw himself down. [On the other hand], if someone pursued him with light blows and he were to arrive at the edge of the roof, reason would judge that the blows were of less significance than the prospect of jumping off, so his limbs would bring him to a stop and he would not be able to throw himself down. For no motivation [2] to do so would be aroused, since the motivation of the will is subservient to the judgment [1] of reason and the senses. Moreover, the power [to act] [3] is subservient to the motivation [2], as is the action itself [4] to the power [to act], while all of these elements are decreed necessarily to an extent to which one is quite unaware. A human being is but the locus and channel for these things, so it could not be the case that they would be from him.[40] So the meaning of his being constrained results from the fact that all of this is produced in him from outside him and not from himself, and the meaning of his being free to choose consists in his being the place in which the will originates in him what is constrained by the judgment of reason—that an action be unqualifiedly good and fitting; so the judgment which emerges has [a dimension of] constraint as well. So constraint is present, even with respect to freedom of choice. Yet the action of fire in burning, for example, is unqualifiedly one of constraint, while the action of God the Most High represents unqualified freedom of choice. So the action of a human being, while it may be constrained in freedom of choice, is on a level between these two.

The party of truth [Ash'arites], looking for a third way of expressing this so that it would constitute a third kind [of action], had recourse to the book of God Most High, and called it *kasb* [lit., acquisition, appropriation].[41] It is not incompatible with constraint [*jabr*] nor with freedom of choice [*ikhtiyār*] but rather comprehends them both, in so far as one understands it. So the action of God the Most High is called "freedom of choice," on condition that freedom of choice is not understood as willing after confusion and indecision, for that would be absurd in His case. In fact, all expressions used in human language are unable to function properly in the case of God Most High, except by way of metaphor or figurative speech. But speaking about that is not suitable for this present inquiry, and would take us far afield.[42]

Here you might object: How can you say that knowledge begets will, that will generates power, and power begets action—in fact, that each originates from what precedes it? For if you say that, you have in effect asserted that something originates outside of the power of God Most High. Yet if you deny it, what sense can we make of the order which obtains from one thing to another? You should know that saying that some things *originate*[43] from others is unqualified ignorance, and the same holds for expressions like 'generate' or others like them, for all of them must be aligned with the intention [*maᶜnā*] expressed by the divine decree [*qudra*]. But this is a principle [*āsl*] which most human beings do not understand, except for "those endowed with real perception" [3:7], who grasp it according to its hidden meaning [*maᶜnā*]. Yet most understand it according to the words alone, with a kind of anthropomorphism [*tashbīh*] adapted to our power, which is far from the truth. But explaining all this would take us too far afield. [What we can say], however, is that certain powers [*maqdurāt*: lit., objects of divine omnipotence] are ordered to others by way of origination [*fi' l-hadūth*] as the conditioned is ordered to its condition. Thus it is that will only emanates from eternal omnipotence after knowledge, and knowledge after life, and life only after the locus of life. Just as one cannot say that life comes from the body, which is the condition of life, the same holds for other levels of orderly arrangement. And while certain conditions may be evident to most people, others will only be apparent to certain specified ones among those to whom such things have been unveiled by the light of truth. In any case, what precedes does precede and what follows does follow only [272] according to truth and necessity, and so it is with all the actions of God Most High.

If that were not so, then preceding and following would amount to a farce, like the action of fools. But even the ignorant acknowledge that God Most High is great and beyond all that, as the saying of the Most High indicates: *I have created jinn and human beings, that they might serve me* [51:56] and again: *We did not create heaven and earth and what lies between them in jest; we did not create them but in truth* [44:38-39]. Now all that is between heaven and earth comes forth in a necessary order that is true and consequent, and it is inconceivable that it be other than it does come forth, according to this order which exists.[44] What follows only follows because it awaits its condition; a conditioned before a condition would be absurd, and absurdity cannot be ascribed to the being of an object of divine omnipotence. Knowledge only follows upon sperm if one supplies the condition of a living thing, and the will which comes after knowledge follows upon sperm only if the condition of knowledge be supplied. All of this offers a way of necessity and the order of truth. There is no room for play or chance in any of this; everything has its rationale and order. Understanding this is difficult, yet our striking out to stop the action of a power in the presence of the power [manifests] the existence of a condition, and offers an example to display the truth in a manner better adapted to the comprehension of weak minds.

This is similar to our considering an unclean human being immersed in water up to his neck. The ritual uncleanness is not removed from his limbs even if the water were able to remove it as it came into contact with them. Now think of the eternal omnipotence present and in contact with objects dependent upon it like the contact of water with limbs, yet in such a way that power is not transmitted to them—just as the ritual uncleanness was not removed by the water for it awaited the condition: cleansing the face. So when the person who is standing in water puts his face in the water, the water acts on the other limbs to remove the ritual uncleanness. But an ignorant person might think that the uncleanness was removed from the hands by virtue of its being removed from the face, because the one produced what followed upon it. Then he would say: the water was in contact [with the limbs] yet nothing was removed [of the uncleanness], yet if the water has not been changed from what it was, how can it now accomplish what it did not accomplish before? For it succeeded in removing the uncleanness from the hands once the face was cleansed, so cleansing the face must remove the uncleanness from the limbs. Now this betrays an ignorance similar to that of one who thinks action is accomplished by the power, that the power [is moved by] the will, and the will by reason—yet that is all wrong.[45] Rather than removing the uncleanness from the face, it is the uncleanness of the hands that is removed by the water coming into contact with them, and not by its cleansing the face. The water is not changed nor is the hand changed, nor is anything produced by them. What is produced is the presence of a condition, and so the influence of a cause is manifested.[46]

In this way you may come to understand the emanation of things so ordained [*muqaddarāt*] from the eternal omnipotence, even though the omnipotent One is eternal and the things ordained [*maqdūrāt*] temporal. But this [train of thought] knocks on another door, to another world of the worlds of unveiling. So let us leave all that, since our aim is to offer counsel regarding the way to faith in divine unity in practice: that the true agent is One, that He is the subject of our fear and our hope, and the One in whom we trust and depend. All that we can mention regarding the seas of faith in divine unity amounts to but a drop from the sea of the third station of the stages of faith in divine unity. But it would be absurd to try to set that out in detail, even with the lifetime of Noah; it would be like trying to remove the water from the sea by taking it out in drops. All of that is contained in the saying: "there is no god but God," but how lightly that falls off the tongue and how easily faith in the meaning of this utterance comes to the heart! Yet how difficult its true reality and its inner kernel even for those *endowed with real perception* [3:7]—so how much more must it be for others!

Diverse dimensions of *agency*

Now you may object: how can there be any common ground between faith in divine unity and the *sharīʿa* [religious law]? For the meaning of faith in divine unity is that there is no agent but God Most High, and the meaning of the law lies in establishing the actions proper to human beings [as servants of God]. And if human beings are agents, how is it that God Most High is an agent? Or if God Most High is an agent, how is a human being an agent? There is no way of understanding 'acting' as between these two agents. In response, I would say: indeed, there can be no understanding when there is but one meaning for 'agent.' But if it had two meanings, then the term comprehended could be attributed to each of them without contradiction, as when it is said that the emir killed someone, and also said that the executioner killed him; in one sense, the emir is the killer and in another sense, the executioner. Similarly, a human being is an agent in one sense, and God—Great and Glorious—is an agent in another. The sense in which God Most High is agent is that He is the originator[47] of existing things [*al-mukhtari' al-mawjud*], while the sense in which a human being is an agent is that he is the locus [*mahal*] in which power is created after will has been created after knowledge has been created, so that power depends on will, and action is linked to power, as a conditioned to its condition.[48] But depending on the power of God is like the dependence of effect on cause, and of the originated on the originator. So everything which depends on a power in such a way as it is the locus of the power is called 'agent' in a manner which expresses that fact of its dependence [273], much as the executioner and the emir can each be called 'killer,' since the killing depends on the power of both of them, yet in different respects. In that way both of them are called 'killer', and similarly, the things ordained [*maqrūrāt*] depend on two powers.

In accordance with that, God Most High in the Qur'an sometimes attributes actions to angels and sometimes to human beings, and at other times applies the very same attributions to Himself. So God Most High says of death: *Say* [*O Muhammad*], *'the angel of death who has charge of you'* [32:11], while the Great and Glorious One also says: *at the point of death God takes human souls* [39:42]; and yet again, in relation to us, *Have you considered the soil you till?* [56:63], yet also: *We have sent the rain in copious downpours and broken up channels in the ground, bringing forth grain there* [80:25-28]. The Great and Glorious One says [of Maryam]: *Then We sent to her Our Spirit who came to her in comely form* [19:17], and then: *We breathed into her of Our Spirit* [21:91]. (But the one breathing [into her] was Gabriel—peace be upon him—as the Most High says: *as We recite it, follow its recital* [75:18]; for it is said in the commentary that this means "when Gabriel recited it to you.") Again, the Most High says: *Kill them! God will punish them by your hands* [9:14], so connecting the killing with them [who carry it out] and the punishment with Himself, yet the killing and the punishment are the same. So the Most High clarifies it, saying: *You* [*Muslims*] *did not kill them, but God killed them*, and further: *You* [*Muhammad*] *did not throw when you threw, but God threw* [8:17]. On the surface this amounts to a denial and an affirmation together, but its meaning is: you did not throw in the sense in which the Lord can be said to throw, since you threw in the sense in which it belongs to a human to throw—and the two senses are different.

As the Most High says: *Who teaches by the pen, teaches man what he knows not* [96:4-5], and again: *The Lord of mercy, He has taught the Qur'an* [55:1-2], and further: *He taught him [man] utterance* [55:4]. Again: *It is Our work to make its meaning clear* [75:19], and *Have you considered what you do in intercourse? Is it you who do the creating, or We?* [56:58-59]. As the Messenger of God—peace be upon him—said in describing the angel of the womb:

"He enters into the womb, taking the sperm in his hand, and then forms it into a body, asking: 'O Lord, masculine or feminine? straight or crooked?' God in turn asked what [the angel] wanted, and created an angel." Or in a variant: "And the angel shaped and then breathed into it the spirit [*ruh*] with happiness or suffering." One of our predecessors said: "the angel who uttered the spirit in him is the same one who inserts spirits into bodies, and he breathes his form into them, so that every breath [*nafs*] one takes is spirit inserted into a body, and in that way is called *spirit*."[49] What is told here by way of a parable of this angel and its description is indeed true, as those who rule over their hearts can testify by their inner vision. For the fact that human beings are composed of spirit is only possible to know from tradition, and any wisdom regarding it without tradition would be pure conjecture.

In a similar way, God Most High spoke in the Qur'an about evidence and signs in earth and heaven: *Does it not suffice you that your Lord is witness over all things?* [41:53], and *God* [*Himself*] *is witness that there is no God but He* [3:18]. Furthermore, it is clear that they are evidence for Himself as well, and that [274] is not contradictory for the paths of demonstration are quite different. Many seekers know God Most High by reflection on existing things, and many [other] seekers know all existing things through God Most High, as the one who remarked: "I have known my Lord through my Lord, and without my Lord I would not know my Lord." This is what the saying of the Most High means by: *Does not your Lord suffice, since He is witness over all things?* [41:53]. God Most High has Himself described what brings to life and makes die, since He entrusted death and life to two angels, and according to the report: "the angels of death and of life were disputing with one another, and the angel of death said: 'I bring the living to death,' while the angel of life retorted: 'I bring the dead to life.' God Most High revealed to both of them: 'Stick to the work entrusted to you to which you have been bound since creation [*as-ṣanʿa*]. I am the one who causes death and brings to life; no one else causes death or brings to life but Me."[50]

So it is that 'acting' is fraught with different senses, and these meanings are not contradictory once you understand [that fact]. As the Prophet ﷺ said to the one to whom he gave some dates: "Take them! Since you did not come to them, they came to you."[51] He made a point of relating the dates with their coming to him, since one knows that dates do not come to someone, but rather that a person comes to them. The Prophet ﷺ responded in a similar way to the penitent who said: "I will turn to God in repentance but I will not turn to Muhammad." Muhammad ﷺ said: "He knows his proper rights."[52] Anyone who relates all there is to God Most High is unquestionably one who knows the truth and the true reality, while whoever relates them to what is other than Him is one whose speech is laced with figurative expressions and metaphors. Figurative expression is on one side while true reality is on another, yet the author of language determined the term 'agent' to mean the one who originates [*mukhtari'*], so those supposing human beings to be originators call them 'agents' according to their power.[53] For they suppose that human beings actualize [*taḥaqiq*], so they imagine [*tawahīm*] that 'agent' is attributed to God Most High metaphorically, as the killing was attributed (in the example) to the emir, yet metaphorically so when contrasted with that attributed to the executioner.

Yet in the measure that the truth is revealed to those inquiring, they will know that things are quite the opposite, and they will say: O linguist, you have posited the term 'agent' to signify the one who originates, but [in that sense] there is no agent but God, so the term belongs properly to Him and metaphorically to whatever is other than Him. That is, you must bear with the way in which linguists have determined it. When the authentic meaning happened to roll off the tongue of a certain Arab [Bedouin], whether intentionally or by chance, the Messenger of God ﷺ gave him his due, saying: "The most apt verse ever spoken by a poet is the saying of Labid: 'Everything except God is empty'."[54] That is, everything which does not subsist in itself, but has its subsistence from another, from the point of view of itself, is nothing. For its truth and its reality comes from another and not from itself, so it is not true essentially [*lā ḥaqq biḥaqīqa*] outside *the Living and the Subsisting* [2:255, 3:2], to Whom *there is no likeness* [42:11], for He subsists essentially [*bidhātihi*] while everything that is other than He subsists by His power. So He is the truly Real One [*al-Ḥaqq*] and all that is other than He is nothing.[55] As Sahl [al-Tustarī] said: "O poor man! He was and you were not, and He will be and you will not be. While you are today, you say: 'I, I'; be now as though you had not been, for He is today as He was."[56]

You may still object: It is now clear that all is coerced [*jabr*]. But if so, what can these mean: reward or punishment, anger or complete approval [*riḍā'*]?[57] How can He be angry at His own deed? You should know that we have already indicated the meaning of that in the Book of Thanksgiving [Book 32 of the *Iḥyā'*], so we will not proceed to a long repetition here. For this has to do with the divine decree [*qadar*], intimations of which we saw with respect to the faith in divine unity which brings about the state of trust in divine providence, and is only perfected by faith in the benevolence and wisdom [of God]. And if faith in divine unity brings about insight into the effects of causes, abundant faith in benevolence is what brings about confidence in the effects of the causes, and the state of trust in divine providence will only be perfected, as I shall relate, by confidence in the trustee [*wakīl*] and tranquillity of heart towards the benevolent oversight of the [divine] sponsor. For this faith is indeed an exalted chapter in the chapters of faith, and the stories about it from the path of those experiencing the unveiling go on at length. So let us simply mention it briefly: to wit, the conviction of the seeker in the station of faith in divine unity, a conviction held firmly and without any doubt. This is a faith deemed to be trustworthy and certain, with no weakness or doubt accompanying it: that when God—Great and Glorious—created all human beings according to a reason greater than reason and a knowledge [275] greater than their knowledge, that He also created for them a knowledge that would sustain each one of them, and bestowed on them a wisdom that they would never cease describing.

In like manner, He enhanced knowledge, wisdom, and reason in a great number of them, and then unveiled for them the effects of things [*al-ʿawāqil al-amūr*], apprising them of the secrets of the intelligible world, teaching them the subtleties of speech and the hidden springs of punishment, to the point where they were thus informed regarding what is good and evil, useful or harmful. Given that He had bestowed reason and wisdom [on them], He then commissioned them to administer the visible and invisible worlds. Even though all of them required direction, it was nonetheless manifest and evident to Him that this would add—may He be praised—to God's direction of creation, in this world and the next. And that direction continues: whether or not the number of atoms be increased or diminished, sickness or evil eye, weakness or poverty or harm will not be removed from those afflicted by them; nor will health, beauty, wealth, or advantage be taken away from those whom God has blessed with them. Indeed, of everything which God Most High created in heaven and earth, if human beings would but turn their eyes to it all and prolong their gaze, they would not see diversity or discontinuity in it. For everything which God Most High distributes among His servants: care and an appointed time [*ajal*], happiness and sadness, weakness and power, faith and unbelief, obedience and apostasy—all of it is unqualifiedly just with no injustice in it, true with no wrong infecting it.

Indeed, all this happens according to a necessary and true order, according to what is appropriate as it is appropriate and in the measure that is proper to it; nor is anything more fitting, more perfect, and more attractive within the realm of possibility.[58] For if something were to exist and remind one of the sheer omnipotence [of God] and not of the good things accomplished by His action, that would utterly contradict [God's] generosity, and be an injustice contrary to the Just One. And if God were not omnipotent, He would be impotent, thereby contradicting the nature of divinity.[59] Indeed, all need and harm in the world, while it represents a deficiency in this world, nonetheless spells an enhancement in the next, and everything which amounts to a deficiency in the next world for one person spells a benefice for another. For if there were no night one would never know the reach of daylight, and absent sickness one would not enjoy good health when one had it; or if there were no hell, the inhabitants of paradise would not know the extent of their blessing. And just as there is no wrong if one is required to sacrifice animal lives as the price of human lives, so the fact that perfection takes precedence over diminishment is proper to justice. Similarly, amplifying blessing on behalf of the inhabitants of paradise while increasing the punishments of the inhabitants of hell, so that the price of the people of faith is paid by the people of unbelief, is quite proper to justice. If diminishment had not been created, the dignity of human beings would not be evident, for perfection and diminishment become evident in relation to one another, so it belongs to generosity and wisdom to create perfection and diminishment together. Just as it is just to cut off an extremity once gangrene has set in, to prolong one's life, because the less perfect is sacrificed to the more perfect, so it is with the order of differences which exist among people in the divisions within this world and the next. All of that is just with no injustice in it; true with no jest in it [cf. 21:16, 44:38].

Now this is another sea immensely deep, with vast extremities and chaotic swells, nearly as extensive as the sea of faith in divine unity, and the boats of those whose capacity is limited flounder in it, for they do not know that this is something hidden, not to be grasped except by those who know. The lore regarding this sea is the secret of the divine decree which confuses the many, and those to whom it has been unveiled are forbidden to disclose its secret. The gist of it is that good and evil are determined by it, and if they were not, then what comes about would have to follow a prior volition in such a way as not to contradict His wisdom and yet not to follow upon His judgment and His command. But everything, small or large, is recorded and carried out by Him according to the divine decree as an object foreseen, and if you were not afflicted you would not make progress, and were you not making progress you would not be afflicted. But let us cut short these allusions to ways of knowing through unveiling which are themselves the basis of the station of trust in divine providence, and return to the knowledge of practices—God Most High willing—and let us praise God and bless the Trustee.[60] [276]

Notes

1. The terms rendered 'stages' [*manāzil*] and 'stations' [*maqāmāt*] are technical terms in Sufi vocabulary marking the way to proximity [*qurb*] with God; see Schimmel, 109-30.

2. The term translated 'state' [*hāl*] represents a Sufi way of speaking of extraordinary states of character in relation to God; see Schimmel, 99, 100, 109-30.

3. The generic term *akhbār* refers to sayings from the tradition, often describing actions or pronouncements of the Prophet ﷺ, collected and published under the specific title of *hadith* [pl. *ahādith*].

4. Qushayrī, *Risala* 75-76, bāb at-tawakkul.

5. Aḥmad b. Hanbal, *Al-musnad* 1,30/1,243, Nr. 205; 1,52/1,313, Nr. 370.

6. ʿIrāqī, *Al-mugnī* 4, 239.

7. Munāwī, *Fayd al-qadīr* 6, 149-150 Nr. 8742.

8. Aḥmad b. Hanbal, *Kitāb az-zuhd* 10.

9. Aḥmad b. Hanbal, *Al-musnad*, 4, 249.

10. Munāwī, *Al-ithāfāt as-sanīya bi-l-aḥādīth al-qudsīya* 99-100, Nr. 229.

11. Abū Nu'aym, *Hilyat al-awliyā' 4.274.*

12. This tradition and those following it come from an anonymous text attributed to Ghazālī: *Mukāsharat al-qulūb al-muqarrib ilā hadrat ʿallam al-ghuyūb*, bab 74 (Cairo 1371/1952, pp. 247-48).

13. Makkī, *Qūt al-qulūb* 2, 90, 19-21 / 3, 123.

14. Qushayrī, *Risāla* 76-77, *bab at-tawakkul.*

15. Spanish translation: *El Justo Medio en la créencia* (Madrid, 1929).

16. A celebrated Qur'anic verse referring to the Prophet's actions at the battle of Badr, where the first Muslim victory was celebrated. For the context, see W. Montgomery Watt, *Muhammad: Prophet and Statesman* (Oxford: Oxford University Press, 1961) 125-26.

17. An Arab proverb, in Freytag, *Arabum Proverbia* 3, 1,276, Nr. 1647.

18. Makkī, *Qūt al-qulūb* 1, 220, 9-10; see Wensinck, *Concordance* 1, 211a-b.

19. Manawi, *Fayd al-qadīr* 4, 534, Nr. 6179.

20. Manawi, *Fayd al-qadīr* 1, 347, Nr. 615.

21. Makkī, *Qūt al-qulūb* 1, 30-32 / 2, 135.

22. On the distinction among these "worlds" see Richard Frank, "Creation and the Cosmic System," 38-46, where he comments on these and other texts; also his *Al-Ghazālī and the Ash'arite School* (Durham NC: Duke University Press, 1994) 36-46. Ghazālī himself will offer some clarifications further on.

23. The "niche of God's light" alludes to Qur'an 24:35, a celebrated verse taken in a mystical sense, and the inspiration for Ghazālī's later *Mishkāt al-anwār*.

24. Gramlich offers another manuscript reading at this point, finding this final expression unclear, yet it seems that Ghazālī wishes to insist that "the power" has no discrimination proper to it, but what is supplied by the intellect.

25. The Sufis often cite this extra-canonical hadith: Sarrāj, *Luma'* 70.

26. For an illuminating description and analysis of *tanzih/tashbih*, see William Chittick and Sachiko Murata, *The Vision of Islam* (Minneapolis MN: Paragon Press, 1996) *passim*.

27. A key hadith; see Aḥmad b. Hanbal, *Al-musnad*, ed. Shākir 13, 152-53; ed. Halabī 2, 251.

28. Maydānī, *Majma' al-amtāl* 2, 172/1, 157; Freytag, *Arabum Proverbia*, 2, 396, Nr. 279.

29. Like *al-Qādir* in the earlier exchange, these are all canonical names of God: *al-Mālik*, *al-Wāhid*, *al-Jabbār*, *al-Qahhār*. cf. Ghazālī, *99 Beautiful Names*, 57-9, 130-31, 66-7, 74.

30. Mālik, *Al-muwatta'* 1, 214, qur'an 31; Wensinck, *Concordance* 1, 304a; for an interpretation, see Ghazālī, *Al-maqsad al-asnā*, 54 [Eng. trans., 42].

31. Gramlich offers the following image corresponding to this expression: whoever comes too late to common prayer stands out from those who are already engaged in the ritual prostrations (535).

32. Hadith: Alī al-Qārī, *Al-asrār al-marfū a fi l-ahbār al-mawdū* a 388.

33. From a verse attributed to Abu Bakr; see Ghazālī, *99 Beautiful Names*, 42.

34. Divine names; cf. Ghazālī, *99 Beautiful Names*, 74.

35. Divine names; cf. Ghazālī, *99 Beautiful Names*, 133-37, which the following closely parallels.

36. An allusion would seem to be the verse cited by Aristotle in *Metaphysics* 12.10 [1076a]: "The rule of many is not good; let one the ruler be."

37. The reference is to Qur'an 20:83-98, 2:45-48, 7:148-49, where the people were misled into crafting a calf to worship in the desert by as-Samiri, "the Samaritan"—cf. SEI 501-2. For the biblical reference, cf. Exodus 32.

38. Contemporaries caught in a "libertatian" picture of willing might refer to Augustine's attempt in *Confessions* (8.viii) to note that we cannot bring ourselves to *will* what we know we should do; a resonance of Romans 7:19-20. For an overview of a classical conception of freedom close to that which al-Ghazālī attempts to articulate here, see my "Freedom and Creation in the Abrahamic Traditions," *International Philosophical Quarterly* 40 (2000) 161-71.

39. The expression here translated as 'motivate' [*dāʿīah*] is treated extensively in Daniel Gimaret, *Théories de l'acte humain en théologie musulmane* (Paris: Vrin, 1980), *passim*, see Index des Termes Techniques, 407.

40. Again, for an account of this "theory of action" involving such "motivations [*dāʿīah*]" see Gimaret (note 39) esp. pp. 143-48, and also Richard M. Frank, "The Autonomy of the Human Agent in the Teaching of ʿAbd al-Jabbar," *Le Muséon* 95 (1982) 323-55, as well as his review of Gimaret in *Biblioteca Orientalis* 39 (1982) 705-15.

41. Cf. M. Schwartz, "'Acquisition' [*kasb*] in Early Kalām," in S.M. Stern and A. Hourani, eds, *Islamic Philosophy and the Classical Tradition* (Columbia SC: University of South Carolina Press, 1972) 355-87; for a comprehensive account of this teaching, generally accepted as *orthodox* in Islam, see Daniel Gimaret, *La doctrine d'al-Ash'arī* (Paris: Cerf, 1990).

42. Here is the point where al-Ghazālī himself calls for an account of analogical language, as later developed by Aquinas; see my "Maimonides, Aquinas and Ghazālī on Naming God," in Peter Ochs, ed., *The Return to Scripture in Judaism and Christianity* (New York: Paulist, 1993) 233-55.

43. The verb *hadatha* is usually reserved for the divine action of creating.

44. On the apparent connections with Ibn Sina here, see Richard M. Frank, *Creation and the Cosmic System: Al-Ghazālī & Avicenna* (Heidelberg: Carl Winter, 1992).

45. This is indeed the order, as we have seen, but the emphasis is on the expression 'accomplished by': Ghazālī has taken pains to insist that the order of creation is suffused with the creator's activity; he is less clear on what we might call "secondary causes," even though his discussion of the respective roles of emir and executioner implies just that. One must carefully distinguish his polemical from his constructive works in this regard: in the *Tahāfut al-Tahāfut* he was intent on deconstructing a pervasive view of causality which left no room for divine initiative; here he can be more constructive, as we shall see. As a result, he can be read in different ways: as in Lenn Goodman, "Did al-Ghazālī Deny Causality?" *Studia Islamica* 47 (1978) 83-120, or in Michael Marmura: "Al-Ghazālī on Bodily Resurrection and Causality," *Aligarh Journal of Islamic Thought* (1989) 46-75.

46. The juridical character of this example begs the question, of course, since the order here described is one explicitly prescribed, whereas we have no independent access to the creator's prescriptions for nature other than our inquiry.

47. This term is not Quranic nor is it a name of God; cf. L.P. Fitzgerald, *Creation in al-Tafsīr al-Kabīr of Fakhr ad-Din al-Rāzī* (Ph.D. dissertation, Australian National University, 1992) 34.

48. Cf. Frank, *Creation and...*, 25.

49. Makkī, *Qūt al-qulūb*, 2, 13, 2-6.

50. ʿIrāqī, *Al-mugni* 4, 251.

51. *Qūt al-qulūb* 2, 14, 4-5 / 3, 20.

52. *Ibid.* 2, 14, 5-6 / 3, 20.

53. This assertion regarding the primary meaningof the term 'agent' reflects the presumption in Ghazālī's Ash'arite milieu that identified *agency* with the activity of creating.

54. *Ibid.* 2, 14, 16-19 / 3, 20.

55. Divine name; cf. Ghazālī, *99 Beautiful Names*, 124-6.

56. *Qut al-qulūb* 2, 6, 29-30 / 3, 9.

57. For the sense of *ridā'*, see Marie-Louise Siauve's translation of *Kitāb al-ḥubb* of the *Iḥyā'*: *Livre de l'amour* (Paris: Vrin, 1986) 247-68.

58. This is Ghazālī's celebrated claim regarding the universe—that it is "the best possible," a claim whose reception has been examined in detail by Eric Ormsby, *Theodicy in Islamic Thought* (Princeton NJ: Princeton University Press, 1984). See also Richard Frank, *Creation...*, 60-61.

59. *al-ʿAdl* [Just] is a name of God (cf. *99 Beautiful Names*, 92-96), and the following expression 'omnipotent' is derived from the name *al-Qādir* (Ibid., 131-32).

60. *al-Wakīl* [Trustee] is a name of God (Ibid., 126).

THE SECOND PART

States of Trust in Divine Providence with Accompanying Practices

This book contains explanations of the state of trust in divine providence [1.], including what the [Sufi] sheikhs say by way of defining such trust [2.]; followed by trust in divine providence with regard to obtaining provisions [3.1], for single persons [3.11] as well as for providers of families [3.12]; with regard to savings [3.2], to repelling injury [3.3], and in connection with removing threats to life by undergoing medical treatment and such practices [3.4]. God is the One who confirms all this by way of His lovingkindness.

[1.] Explicating the State of Trust in Divine Providence

We have already mentioned that the station of trust in divine providence consists of knowledge, states [of the soul], and practices; and [the connection with] knowledge has been discussed. When it is realized, such trust consists in a stable state [of the soul—*hāl*], with knowledge as its root [*asl*] and practice its fruit. Many have already embarked on the task of elucidating the definition of trust in divine providence and come up with various opinions. For each of them was writing from his own particular standpoint, relating his definition according to Sufi practice, so there is no point in disseminating that. Let us rather remove the cover from it by saying: *tawakkul* [trust in divine providence] is derived from *wakāla* [power of attorney, management]. It is said: he entrusted his affairs to someone, that is: he commissioned that one to take care of them, depending on him to do it. And the one so entrusted is called *wakīl* [trustee, authorized representative, agent], the one commissioned, *muttakil*, or *mutawakkil ʿayayh* [the one to be depended upon], in the measure that one's soul is at peace with regard to him and one is confident in him, nor can one suspect the least thing of him or believe there to be any weakness or deficiency in him. So trust of this sort [*tawakkul*] consists in the heart's relying on the trustee [*wakīl*] alone.

Let us focus on the role of a *wakīl* [trustee, authorized representative, agent] in litigation, for example. If someone has had false or dubious charges brought against him, and entrusts the case to one who will expose their dubiety, then that person will be the one upon whom he depends [*mutawakkil*] , the one in whom he has confidence and in whom his soul can be at peace in entrusting itself to him. But this will be the case only if he can be convinced of four things about him: that he be nothing but rightly guided, exquisitely able and powerful, flawlessly eloquent, and utterly compassionate. Regarding right guidance, it will show him how to confront the dubious charge to the point where nothing at all of its devious power will be hidden from him. Regarding power and ability, he will be emboldened to speak the truth clearly, without dissimulation, fear, embarrassment or cowardice. In that way, he may be able—in the face of the dubious charge of the adversary—to expose the fear or cowardice, shame or other such attitudes which are diverting his heart from coming clean about the matter. Regarding eloquence, it is a power as well, albeit in the tongue, by which one can clearly articulate everything which the heart emboldens him to say. For not everyone who knows how to confront dubious charges will be able to unravel the tangle of dubious charges by the eloquence of his speech.

Regarding his being utterly compassionate, this is what moves [the attorney] to do everything he possibly can on his client's behalf. For without solicitude for his client, his powers will hardly suffice, for he will fail to concern himself with his affairs, nor will it be of any interest to him whether the adversary wins or not, or whether his client's case fails or not through his actions. For if it were the case that the plaintiff was endowed with these four characteristics or even one of them, or it happened that his adversary surpassed him in all four of them, [the defendant's] soul could hardly be at peace with regard to his attorney. Quite the contrary, his heart would become disquieted and filled with concern for the legal stratagems and arrangements needed to get the better of all he had to fear—given the deficiencies of his attorney and the attacks of his adversary. Certainly there would be differences in degree of his states of shattered confidence and peace of mind according to the different levels of strength in his [original] conviction regarding his attorney's possession of these qualities.

Now convictions and impressions regarding strength and weakness will differ in countless ways, and the states of trusting in power to bring calm and confidence differ endlessly up to the limit of certainty [*yaqīn*] which [277] never wanes. Take the case where the trustee is the father of the one entrusting, so that he would be the one named in everything permitted or prohibited regarding him. So the child would have certainty regarding the extent of his compassion and concern, thereby inducing one quality of the four mentioned. Similarly, one can imagine him lacking the rest of the qualities, yet after long and persistent experience and practice, he could become more proficient in expressing himself to people eloquently and more powerful than they in giving explanations as well as in defending the truth—but also in making the true seem to be false and the false seem to be true.[1]

If you can come to know what trust [*tawakkul*] is from this parable, use it to aspire to trust in God Most High. For if you assert in your soul, either by the way of unveiling or by a decisive conviction, that there is no agent but God, as we have insisted; and you are convinced along with that of the perfection of [His] knowledge and power to meet all the needs of human beings, and then of the perfection of [His] solicitude, sympathy and lovingkindness towards human beings as a whole and individually—and that no power surpasses the reach of His power, no knowledge the range of His knowledge, nor does any solicitude or lovingkindness exceed what He has for you—then entrust your heart without hesitation to Him alone, without inclining at all to anything other than Him, nor to one's own self, one's own might or strength. For there is no might or strength but God's, as we have insisted, in [the section on] faith in divine unity, where we spoke of action and power, for might is the same as action, and strength the same as power.

If you cannot find this state in yourself, that could be a result of one or another factor. Either a diminishment of certitude with respect to one of these four qualities, or a weakness in the heart, a kind of illness by which cowardice takes possession of it and troubles it with fantasies overpowering it. Yet the heart is naturally susceptible to being aroused by fantasies and yielding to them, yet without any diminution of certainty: so that if one is offered honey, yet when set before him it appears to be mud, his nature might well reject it; in fact, it would be difficult for him to accept it. Or if a reasonable person were assigned to spend the night in the company of a corpse in a casket or on a blanket or even in the house, his nature would revolt at the thought even though he be certain that the man was dead—indeed stiff with *rigor mortis*, and the *sunna* of God Most High[2] was in force that he not rise nor be brought to life now (even though He be able to do so); just as that same *sunna* saw to it that the pen in his hand would not turn into an animal, nor the cat into a lion—though [God] has the power to do so. Yet even though one be secure in these certainties, his nature would revolt at the prospect of sleeping on a blanket with a corpse, or spending the night with it in the house—even though it would hardly revolt at the presence of other inanimate bodies. That is a cowardice of the heart, a kind of weakness that human beings can scarcely be so free from that they do not have a little of it, and it can even be so strong as to become an illness to the point of one being afraid to spend the night in a house alone even though the door be securely bolted.

So we may conclude that trust in divine providence will not be complete without both strength of heart and strength of certainty together, for both of them contribute to achieving tranquillity and peace of heart. Indeed tranquillity of heart is one thing, and certainty quite another, for many who are certain are not thereby at peace, as the Most High said to Abraham—peace be upon him: "What, and you do not believe? Yes, but would that my heart be at peace" [2:260]. He was asking that he might see the raising of the dead with his eyes to fix it in his imagination, since the soul follows the imagination and rests in it. But it will not rest in a certitude based on declarations about such things until it has attained the last of the stages of a "soul at peace" [89:27], and that can never be at the beginning. Furthermore, many can be at peace without possessing certainty, as it is with those participating in other religions or following different paths. Jews are at peace in their hearts being Jews, as are Christians as well, but they have no certainty at all. "For they follow conjecture and what their souls incline them to even though guidance has come to them from their Lord,"[3] and that guidance would have been the ground of certainty, if they had not turned away from it.

Since cowardice and courage are instinctual, they cannot contribute to certainty, so they are one of the factors [*āsbāb*] impeding the state of trust in divine providence, just as another factor is a diminution of certitude in the four qualities. Yet when these qualities do come together, they become factors in attaining confidence in God Most High. As one has said: "It is written in the Torah: 'cursed by one who places his confidence in a man like him';" and as the Prophet ﷺ said: "God Most High will humble whoever seeks strength through [his] servants."[4]

Now that the meaning of trust in divine providence has been unveiled for you, so that you know the state that is called *tawakkul*, you should know that this state has three stages of strength and weakness. We have already considered the first stage, which is the state of one who, with respect to God Most High, is confident in His security and solicitude in a manner similar to the state of one who places his confidence in a trustee [*wakīl*]. The second stage is stronger yet; it is the state of one who comports himself with God Most High as a child with his mother: he knows no one other than her, he takes refuge in no [278] one other than her, and relies only on her. When he sees her, he hangs onto the hem of her skirt in every situation and never lets her go. If misfortune strikes him in her absence, the first thing to fall from his lips is "mother," just as the first desire to stir in his heart is for his mother, for she is his refuge. For he is already confident in her security and her sufficiency and her compassion—a confidence not without some keen sense of discrimination connected with it.

All this is considered to be natural when it comes to childhood, but if one were to seek an elucidation of this quality, one would be unable to talk about it or bring its fine points to mind. For all of this lies beyond [our] perception, yet whoever gives his attention to God—Great and Glorious—reflects upon Him and relies on Him, sets his heart on Him [lit., falls in love with Him] as the child sets his heart on his mother, is truly one who trusts in divine providence, as the child inclines trustingly to his mother.

The difference between this stage and the first is that this trusting person has already become totally absorbed by his trusting, in such a way that his heart is not inclined to the reality of trusting itself, but rather to the One alone in whom it places its trust. For there is no room in his heart for anyone other than the One in whom it puts its trust. The first one, on the other hand, places his trust in the inclination and what he gains from it [*kasb*], so he is not detached from his own trusting because this inclination to trusting is *his* as well as the awareness of it, and that keeps the one so engaged from gazing uniquely at the One in whom he places his trust. Sahl [at-Tustarī] was speaking of this stage when someone asked him what the lowest [stage] of *tawakkul* would be. He responded: "Leaving security behind." And the middle stage? "Leaving freedom of choice behind," which was his comment on [our] second stage. And when he was asked about the highest stage, Sahl would not speak of it, but rather said that he only knew people who had attained the middle one.[5]

The third stage is the highest: it is to be in the presence of God Most High, whether active or at rest, like a corpse in the hands of the one washing it,[6] differing only in that while one regards oneself to be dead, the eternal omnipotence moves one to action, as the hand of the one washing it moves the corpse. Such a one is confirmed in his certainty by the fact that he is a channel for action, willing, knowing, and other attributes, in such a manner that nothing happens by constraint, for any expectations regarding how things will proceed with him will be made known clearly. Such a one differs from the child, for the child takes refuge in his mother, cries and hangs onto the hem of her skirt, running after her; but this one is rather like a child who knows that his mother is looking for him whether he screams for her or not, that she is carrying him whether he hangs on the hem of her skirt or not, and that she will extend her breast to him and give him to drink whether he asks for milk or not. This station of trust in divine providence results in one's leaving petitionary prayer and asking behind him, confident in His magnanimity and solicitude, and that he will be given an invitation more gracious than he could have asked for. For how many are the blessings which began before asking and praying, and indeed without one's being worthy of them! The second stage did not require leaving prayer and petition behind; it only required that one cease asking anyone but Him alone.

Now you might ask: how can one imagine these states actually coming about? You should know that all this is not impossible but it is exceedingly rare, and while the second and third are more cherished, the first is closer to what is possible. So even when the second or third occur, it is hardly likely that they will last; in fact, the third stage will hardly last as long as the pallor on the face of a frightened person. That the heart expands in glancing at such power and strength and other factors is natural, while its contraction is accidental, just as it is natural for blood to expand into all the arteries and accidental for it to recede from them. To be frightened means that the blood completely recedes from a person's face to the point where the redness that had been visible behind the thin veil of his skin vanishes from his face. The skin is a thin veil behind which can be seen the redness of the blood, so that its contraction results in the pallor, but that does not last. Similarly the complete contraction of the heart upon glancing at the power and strength and other factors clearly cannot last. And the second stage is like the pallor of a feverish person, which hardly lasts more than a day or two, while the first is like the pallor of a sick person so confirmed in his illness that it is neither unusual for it to last or for it to cease.[7]

Now you might ask: how is it that a person could continue to depend on factors [worldly causes] in these states? You should know that the third station completely eschews planning, so long as it lasts and prevails, while those participating in it are like someone quite bewildered. The second station eschews all planning except what relates to taking refuge in God by prayer and supplication, like the infant's "planning" to depend on his mother alone. The first state, however, in no way rejects planning or freedom of choice, although it does eschew certain forms of planning, as in the example of one's entrusting his lawsuit to his attorney: he left his planning in the hands of another, his attorney. He did not, however, relinquish planning what to say to his attorney about it, or the planning which he knew [his attorney would carry out] by custom and practice, without having to instruct him about it specifically. What he makes known to him by instructing him consists in saying to him: "Let it be that I shall only speak [about the lawsuit] in your presence;" and in doing that he is certainly involved in planning when he is in his presence. But this is not inconsistent with his entrusting [the case] to him, for he does not rely on him because of his own strength or his own power to make clear arguments, nor is he [279] relying on the power of anyone other [than the attorney]. Yet it belongs to the perfection of his trusting in him that [the one entrusted] does what he has prescribed for him to do; for if he were not able to be trusted to do that, or if one could not rely on his word, his word would no longer testify to his character [lit., he would not longer be present in his word].

Regarding the things known from custom and habitual practice [*sunna*], one of them that he would know from custom [*ᶜādah*] is that the adversary is only obliged to documents, so perfect trust in [one's lawyer] would leave that to him. For all that would depend on his practice and his custom, in line with what they require, as he is the one who must handle the documentation himself as the case unfolds. So present planning is indispensable, as is planning to prepare documents, and if he were to fail to do any of that, then one's trust [in him] would be diminished, but how could it be so when he fulfills it? Indeed, once it is apparent that he fulfills instructions, prepares documents, is attentive to practice and to custom, and so remains master of his arguments, then [the one who has entrusted himself to him] will end up nearly at the second or third station while in his presence, to the point of standing by like a bewildered onlooker, unable to rely on his own power or might, since he has no power or might left. In fact, he had already entrusted himself to his advocate's power and might, while in his presence, as well as in preparing documents according to the advocate's instructions and practice. So he has reached his limit, and all that is left to him is peace of soul and confidence in his advocate as he awaits what will transpire.

If you reflect on this, every ambivalence you have felt concerning trust in God's providence will be removed, and you will understand that renouncing all planning or activity is not a condition of such trust, but rather that no planning or activity can take place at all without such trust. Indeed, it reaches to the very joints and subsequent details of our activities, so that when the one entrusting relies on his own power and might to be present and make preparations, that is not inconsistent with trusting, because he knows that, were it not for the advocate's being present, his presence and his preparations would be absurd and by their very nature futile. It would be futile insofar as his power and might were involved, but in the measure that the advocate prosecutes [the case], bolstered by his arguments, and instructing him by his counsel and practice, then the only power and might operative will be that of the advocate.

This example, however, does not make complete sense with regard to the advocate in question, because he is not the creator of his power or his strength. He is rather the one who puts them to use, for if he did not do that, they would be of no benefit at all.[8] But what can be affirmed of the authentic advocate [*al-Wakīl*], namely God Most High, is that He is creator of power and of strength (as we have already noted in treating faith in divine unity (in part I); and that He is the One who makes both of them function since He constitutes both of them as conditions for what He will create [so that it happens] after both of them [occur], by way of utility and intention. So there is no power or strength except in God, the true and righteous One[9], and whoever sees this to be the case has exquisite rewards coming to him—those related in the traditions concerning everyone who says: "There is no power or strength but in God."[10]

Now that might appear to be outrageous, so one could say: how can one give this expression such total praise when it comes so easily to the lips, and the heart is so easily convinced by what it understands of these words? But how far from the mark that is! This is simply the response to that vision which we expounded in the treating of faith in divine unity. For this expression, with the praise associated with it, is closely related to the expression "there is no god but God," while praising it is like associating the two meaning with each other. So by this expression two things—power and strength—are connected with God Most High alone, and the expression "there is no god but God" relates them both to Him. Clarify the differences between everything and these two things, and you will know how the acclamation "there is no god but God" is connected with this [statement "there is no power or strength but in God"]. As we spoke earlier, in treating faith in divine unity, of two shells and two kernels, so it is with this expression and all other expressions. Most human beings are limited to the outer two shells and do not follow the path to the inner kernels, but the saying of the Prophet—peace be upon him—concerns the two kernels: "paradise surely belongs to whoever says 'there is no god but God' with a sincere and pure heart."[11] While he had stated it without mention of righteousness and purity of heart, he wanted to add this restriction to the general statement, since forgiveness is connected with faith and pious works in certain places [in the tradition], and to pure faith in others, so he intended to add pious works as a restriction.[12] For sovereignty [over oneself] is not attained by talking, for moving the tongue is speech, and contracting the heart is speech as well—albeit speech of the soul; yet righteousness and purity of heart are well beyond both of these.

Only those who are drawing close [to Him] in purity of heart will be established on the throne of sovereignty, though whoever draws near to them in degree, by participating in certainty, also belongs to the stages of relating to God Most High, even if they do not arrive at that of sovereignty. Do you not see that God—may He be praised—spoke in the *sura* "the Great Event" of those who came before, the ones who draw near, entering upon the throne of sovereignty:

"on thrones decorated, reclining on them, facing one another" [56:15-16]. To the extent that one arrives at a participation in certainty, however, there is no more talk [280] of water, shadows, fruits, trees, or wide-eyed houris, for all of that belongs to pleasures of seeing, drinking, eating, and marriage; yet while such things may conceivably last for animals, how far it is from animal pleasure to the pleasure of sovereignty, or from entering into the highest of the uppermost heavens in the company of the Lord of those who know [Muhammad]! If these earthly pleasures were the ones decreed, they would not extend beyond animals, nor would the ranks of angels rise above them. Or do you think that the states of animals—the same as those present in sports: enjoyment of water, drinking, and forms of eating crowned by violent outburst and copulation—are higher and give greater pleasure, are nobler and more fitting and blessed? Do you suppose that such states belong to the states of angels in their happiness, close to the company of the Lord of those who know in the highest of the uppermost heavens? How far from the mark! What could be farther from a [correct] grasp than someone [wondering] whether it was better to be an ass or in the rank of Gabriel—peace be upon him—or even to prefer the rank of an ass to that of Gabriel!

It is hardly a secret that each thing is like that to which it is attracted: a soul which inclines itself more to the craft of shoemaking than it is inclined to the art of writing is in its substance more like a shoe than a book. Similarly, if one yearns in his soul in such a way that he inclines to the pleasure of animals rather than yearning so that he inclines towards the pleasures of angels, he will inevitably become more like an animal than an angel. These are the ones of whom it is said: *they are like cattle; nay, they are in worse errors* [7:179]. They are in worse error because cattle do not have it in their power to aspire to the rank of angels; all they have to aspire to is aging! Yet for human beings, it is in their power to aspire [to the rank of angels], and one who is capable of inclining towards perfection is more deserving of censure and more appropriately reminded of his error—provided both these [reproofs] do not hinder his [actually] aspiring to perfection. But all this talk is quite beside the point, so let us return to our purpose, which is to explain the meaning of the saying "there is no god but God" as well as the meaning of the saying "there is no power or might except God's," and [to insist] that unless one can utter them from inner vision [*mushāhada*], one can hardly attain the state of trust in divine providence.

Now you might query: all that you have done in saying "there is no power or might but God's" is to relate two things to God Most High. What if the saying were "God created the heavens and the earth"? Would praising that saying be like praising the other? To which I would reply: no; for praise answers to the rank of that to which praise is due, and there is no parity in rank between these two [sets of things being related to God]. Nor can one call attention to the greatness of the heavens and earth and to the smallness of power and might—if it be permitted to speak of smallness with respect to these two attributes [of God], for this is hardly a matter of the bulk of individual items! Quite the contrary, everyone knows that the earth and the heavens do not belong to human affairs but are part of the creation of God Most High, whereas the Mu'tazilites and the philosophers, and many other factions, have quite obscured the two objects, power and might. In fact, they invite one to refine one's speculation in opinion and reasoning to the point of splitting hairs on the fine edge of their speculation, but this is dangerously destructive and a gross error, leading those who are unaware to their ruin. For they assert these to be two things in themselves, and such an assertion amounts to diluting [*shirk*] faith in divine unity by acknowledging a creator other than God Most High [namely, an attribute].

But for those who overcome this obstacle to the grace of God Most High, their place will be higher and their rank greater, for they are the righteous ones, saying: "there is no power or might but God's." For as we have already noted, there are but two obstacles to faith in divine unity. The first is to focus one's attention on the heavens and the earth, the sun and the moon, stars, clouds and rain, and other inanimate bodies. The second is to fix one's attention on the free choice of animals, and it is the greater and more dangerous of the two obstacles; yet perfecting the secret of faith in divine unity means overcoming both of them. And thence comes the signal praise for this expression, that is, praise for the inner vision [*mushāhada*] which this expression translates. So the state of faith in divine unity resolves to disavowing power and might [as though they were attributes distinct from God], and trusting in the One, the True.[13] This will become clear once we have set down specific actions connected with trust in divine providence—God Most High willing!

[2.] Explanation of What [Sufi] Sheikhs Have Said about the States of Trust in Divine Providence

While nothing which will be explicated ranges beyond what we have treated, nonetheless each one has something to say of specific states. Abū Mūsā ad-Daybulī said: "I asked Abū Yazīd [al-Bistāmī] what trust in divine providence was. He answered: 'What are you asking?' I said: 'Our companions say: if vipers and lions were on your right and your left, would not your inner self be agitated at that?' To which Abū Yazīd responded: 'Indeed, that is very close; yet were the people of paradise to enjoy their lot, and the people [281] of hellfire to suffer in the fire, and it were incumbent upon you to distinguish between the two, that would lie outside the domain of trust in divine providence'."[14] The saying which Abū Mūsā mentioned related to the most sublime of all states of trust, the third station. What Abū Yazīd said to him touches on the most penetrating sort of knowledge, which is one of the roots of trust in divine providence, knowledge of [divine] wisdom: that which God Most High does He does by necessity [*bi'l wājib*], for He does not discriminate between the people of hellfire and the people of paradise in consideration of a principle of justice and wisdom—and that is utterly mysterious![15]

Now the sort of knowledge behind this is the secret of the divine decree, and Abū Yazīd seldom said anything about the highest of the stations or the most exalted of the ranks, yet laying aside caution with respect to serpents is hardly a condition of the first station of trust! Indeed, Abū Bakr—the one in whom God is pleased—took care when he was in a cave to keep a serpent from coming in: although it does say that he used his foot to do this, and that his inner self was not agitated on account of it. But it is also said that he did it out of compassion, for the sake of the Messenger of God ﷺ, and not for his own sake.[16] Trust in divine providence only disappears in the presence of agitation and alteration of one's inner self to the extent that the matter concerns oneself. With regard to that, I shall explain later on that situations of this sort, and many others as well, are not inconsistent with such trust. For the movement of one's inner self in the face of a serpent is fear, and it is right for one who trusts in divine providence to fear the power of the serpent, since the serpent has no power or might except God's, so exercising caution is not to place one's trust in one's own planning or power and might to take care, but rather in the creator of power and might and planning.

When Dhū al-Nūn al-Misrī was asked about trust in divine providence, he answered: "Repudiation of masters and renunciation of means [*āsbāb*]." Repudiation of masters refers to the knowledge of faith in divine unity, while renunciation of means refers to actions. This need not keep one from clarifying the state, so long as what he said requires it. So they said to him: tell us more. So he said: "Cast the soul into servitude and so deliver it from being master"—and this refers to complete freedom from power and might.[17] When Hamdūn al-Qassār was asked about trust in divine providence, he responded: "If you had ten thousand dirhams and were one-sixth of a dirham in debt, you could not be sure whether you would die with your debt around your neck. And if you were ten thousand dirhams in debt with no provision to remit it at death, do not abandon hope that God Most High would absolve you from it."[18] This refers to purity of faith in the range of [divine] omnipotence: that among the determinations of that power [*maqdūrāt*] are hidden factors [*āsbāb*] beyond those obvious to us.

When Abū dullāh Qurashī was asked about trust in divine providence, he said: "Dependence on God Most High in every situation," When the one asking him said: tell us more, he said: "Leaving every means [*sabab*] behind, or using means to attain to the True One; to that extent is one trusting."[19] The first comprises three stations while the second refers to the third station specifically, and it can be compared to (Abraham's ﷺ trust in God—when Gabriel—peace be upon him—said to him "Do you need anything?" and he answered:) "From you, no."[20] For his asking would be a means leading to a means, that is to Gabriel's protection of him; while renouncing even asking [showed his] confidence that God Most High, if He wished, would put Gabriel at his service—so trusting was Abraham ﷺ.

Amazingly enough, this state is hidden even from oneself in God Most High: that one sees nothing other than God. It is a state rare in itself, and so rare that it should last [even if it occurs], that it is unlikely that it ever exists!

Abū Sa'īd al-<u>Kh</u>arrāz said: "Trust in divine providence is violence without tranquillity and tranquillity without violence."[21] Perhaps he is referring to the second station here, for tranquillity without violence refers to tranquillity of heart in the Advocate [*al-Wakīl*] and confidence in Him, while violence without tranquillity refers to his taking refuge in Him, supplicating Him, and imploring Him in His presence, as the child does violence to his mother yet is tranquil in his heart regarding her perfect compassion. Abū ʿAlī ad-Daqqāq said: "Trust in divine providence has three stages: trust, surrender [*taslīm*], and commitment [*tafwīd*]. The one who entrusts is tranquil in his promise, the one who surrenders is replete in his knowledge, and the one who has committed himself content in his judgment."[22] This refers to the different stages, considering them in connection with what is seen in them, for knowledge is the basis, promise follows upon it, and judgment follows upon promise. One is not far from attaining to the heart of one who trusts in divine providence by looking at matters in this way. So far as the Sufi sheikhs on trust in divine providence, there are other sayings than the ones we have mentioned, but we will not prolong this, for the unveiling is more profitable from [282] the stories and traditions themselves. Such are the implications of the state of trust in divine providence, with God confirming it by His compassion and grace.

[3.] Explanation of the Actions of Those Who Trust in Divine Providence

You should know that knowledge brings about the state, and the state results in actions. It has been supposed that the meaning of such trust is to forego provision for the body and keep the heart from planning, and to collapse on the ground like someone feeble-minded by the roadside, or a piece of meat on the butcher-block—but this is only what ignorant people suppose. For that is prohibited [*harām*] by religious law; and if religious law commends one who trusts in God, how could this station undermine the station of religion by acts prohibited by religion? So we shall remove the coverings from this subject and speak about how the effects of trust in divine providence are manifest in actions of human beings and in the range of their knowledge and their goals. For human beings are moved by their free choice to [3.1] obtaining something beneficial to them which they lack, like provisions; or to [3.2] protecting what is beneficial, as in storing provisions; or to [3.3] keeping harm from touching them, as in repulsing attackers, thieves, or predatory animals; or to [3.4] removing harm already present from them, as in being cured from illness. The goals of human actions do not exceed these four kinds: obtaining or protecting what is beneficial, and repulsing or removing harm. So let us speak about the conditions of trust in divine providence, and its stages, according to each one of these aims, together with the witness of revelation.

[3.11] *On obtaining what is beneficial for single persons*

We say that there are three degrees of means by which one obtains what is beneficial: [a] those that are always reliable, [b] those that are presumed to work, with a presumption in which one is confident, and [c] those which one imagines might work, by a fantasy in which the soul cannot confide itself with perfect confidence nor can it be at peace with it. The first degree: means that are always reliable. These are those in which other means following after them are arranged according to the planning of God and His will in an uninterrupted and invariant order. This is like having a meal put before you when you are hungry and need it, yet you did not lift a finger to prepare it, so you say: "I am one who trusts in God, and the condition of such trust is renouncing effort. Lifting a hand to do it would be effort and action, like chewing it with the teeth and swallowing it, in accordance with the palate being higher than the digestive organs." But this is pure idiocy and has nothing to do with trust in divine providence. If you were to wait for God Most High to create satiety in you without bread, or to create in bread a motion towards you, or to enjoin an angel to chew it for you and see that it reaches your stomach—that would simply display your ignorance of the practice [*sunna*] of God Most High. As would your not sowing seed in the ground yet hoping that God Most High would create plants without seeds, or thinking that your wives would give birth without intercourse, as Mary—praise be to her—gave birth. All of that is idiocy, yet stories of this sort abound to the point that it would be impossible to count them.

At this station, trust in divine providence does not consist in actions but in a state and in knowledge. The knowledge consists in your knowing that God Most High created food, hands, human beings, power, and action; and that He is the one who feeds you and gives you to drink. The state consists in your heart's being tranquil and your depending on the action of God Most High rather than on hands or food. Indeed, how can you depend on the soundness of your hand when you may suddenly become agitated or become paralyzed? How can you depend on your power when something could happen to you quite suddenly that would take away your reason and so nullify your power of action? Or how can you depend on making food available, when God Most High could keep you from attaining it or incite animals to rouse you from your dwelling and so cut you off from your food? Since such things are possible and there is no cure for them but the grace of God Most High, you had best be pleased with that and rely on it. Once one has reached this state and this knowledge, let him lift his hand and thereby be one who trusts in divine providence!

The second degree: Means which are not certain yet see to it that the factors following them do not occur without them, even though it is possible that they could take place without them, albeit infrequently. Consider those who leave cities and caravans to travel in desert wastes where people rarely go, and undertake their travel without taking along any provisions—this cannot be a condition for trusting in divine providence. Rather, taking along provisions for the desert is the custom of holy people [lit., friends of God], and that does not nullify trust in divine providence so long as one depends on God Most High and not on the provisions, as we have said before. In fact, such activity is permissible, and belongs to the highest of the stations of trust in God, for [Ibrahim] al-Hawwās acted so. However, you might say: this leads one to destruction or plunges one into destruction.[283] But you should know that two conditions keep such [provisioning] from being prohibited. First, that it behooves a person to train his soul, to do battle against it and to put it in order by refraining from food for a week or nearly so, to the point that refraining from it does not weary the heart, confuse the mind, or make it difficult to carry out remembrace of [*dhikr*] God Most High. The second is to be able to nourish oneself with plants or whatever humble thing lies at hand. Given both these conditions, one will not fail to handle things in the desert, should he meet each week with another person or reach an encampment or a dwelling or the grass that he needs to live in order to struggle against himself.

For battling against oneself is the basis of trusting in divine providence, and [Ibrahim] al-Hawwās and others who trusted like him have relied on it. The proof of this is that al-Hawwās was never without a needle, scissors, rope, and a long-handled pot; and he said: "this does not violate trust in God."[23] The reason is that he knew that water in the desert is not to be found on the surface of the ground, and that it is not the normal practice [*sunna*] of God Most High that water come up from a well without a bucket and rope, or that one could manage to find a bucket or rope in the desert in the way one could manage to find grass. One needs water for ritual ablution several times a day, and for thirst once each day or two days, but because of the body heat of movement, a traveler cannot do without water, even if he may refrain from food. Similarly, he has but one cloak, and should that tear, his nakedness would be uncovered; yet he would not find needle or scissors in the desert, as the normal result of ritual prayer, nor could one expect there to be two separate establishments for sewing and cutting materials—something one hardly finds in the desert!

Everything which is contained in the meaning of these four things is also connected with the second degree [of relating to means], because it considers what is a purported rather than a sure means. For it could happen that his cloak would not be torn or that someone would give him a cloak, or that he would find someone at the brink of the well to give him a drink; whereas it will not happen that the food will move itself inside him masticated! There are differences between the two degrees, yet the second is contained with the meaning of the first, as we shall indicate.

If one were isolated in one of the ravines of a mountain in such a way that there were no water or grass, and no traveler came upon him there, yet he were to sit down to trust in God, he would thereby be a sinner, bringing about his own destruction. It would be like the story of the ascetic, who left the city and stayed at the foot of a mountain for a week, saying: "I will not ask for a single thing until my Lord gives me something to sustain me." A week passed and he was about to die, for no one gave him any sustenance. So he said: O Lord, if you are to keep me alive, give me the sustenance which you have set aside for me, and if not, take me to yourself." To which the great God responded, by way of inspiration: "By my strength! We will not give you any sustenance until you enter the city and sit there among the people." So he entered the city and sat there, and one person came to him with food and another with drink. He ate and drank, and became apprehensive within himself because of that. Then God Most High revealed to him: "Did you want to attain to my wisdom with your asceticism in the world? Did you not know that providing for my servants by the hands of my servants is dearer to me than providing by the hand of my power?"

So the renunciation of all means is contrary to His wisdom, and amounts to ignorance with respect to God Most High, whereas acting according to the necessities of the practice [*sunna*] of God Most High, while placing one's trust in God—Great and Glorious—and not in means, is not inconsistent with trusting in divine providence—as we emphasized earlier by the story of the attorney in the trial. Yet means are divided into manifest and hidden ones, and for the meaning of trust in divine providence, the hidden means will suffice without the manifest ones, while the soul finds its tranquillity in the cause which makes them to be means [i.e., the Creator] rather than in the means [themselves].

You might ask: what do you say about one who sits at home without earning his livelihood? Is that prohibited, permissible, or recommended?[24] You should know that it cannot be prohibited because it is like the activity of Sufis wandering in the desert, and that did not destroy them; yet doing something prohibited should be destructive of one's very self. Moreover, it is not unlikely that he will be given food "in a way that he does not foresee" [65:3], even though it may be late in coming to him; yet he can be patient until that happens. On the other hand, if he were to have locked the door of the house behind him so that there were no way anyone could come to him, such an action would be prohibited. But if he opened the door of the house yet did nothing, neither devoting himself to prayer nor to earning his livelihood, it would be more appropriate for him to go out [into the world]. But his action is, in any case, not prohibited, unless he were near death; in which case he would have to go out to pray or to earn his livelihood. But if his heart is absorbed in God, unconcerned with people and not looking for anyone to enter the house and give him anything to eat, but rather looking forward to the grace of God Most High and thereby absorbed in God, he is indeed blessed [284] and in one of the stations of trust in God.

That station consists in one's being absorbed in God Most High and not concerned with one's own sustenance, for sustenance will invariably be given him. As a certain learned person rightly said of that station: "So it is with a man: if he runs away from his sustenance, it will seek him out; so if he were to flee from death it would catch up with him. And if one were to ask God Most High not to sustain him, He would not pay any attention. For the man would be a sinner, and God would say to him: 'you ignorant one; how could I create you and not sustain you'?"[25] And Ibn Abbās—may God be pleased with both of them—also spoke about that: "People differ about everything except about sustenance and the appointed time [*ajal*: term of one's life], for they agree that only God gives sustenance and decides [the time of] one's death."[26] The Prophet—peace be upon him—said: "If you entrust yourselves to God, your trust will be authentic and He will give you sustenance as he sustains the birds who leave in the morning with empty stomachs and return replete in the evening; so at your prayer withdraw to the mountains."[27] And Jesus—peace be upon him—said: "Look at the birds! They do not sow or reap or store things away, and God Most High gives them their sustenance each day. And if you say: we have larger stomachs, then look at the wild animals and how God Most High has determined specifically for their sustenance."[28] Abū Ya'qūb as-Sūsī said: "Those who trust in God receive their sustenance from the hands of men without burdening them, while others are preoccupied and exhausted."[29] Yet another of them said: "All men are beholden to God Most High for their sustenance, but some of them, like beggars, eat in humiliation; others with effort and anxiety, like merchants; still others with indignity, like laborers; others with strength, like the Sufis, looking to the Eminent One [*al-Azīz*] and receiving their sustenance from His hand without concern for means."[30]

The third degree is connected with means which one imagines to be linked with what follows from them, yet with no clear confidence, as with one who examines with intricate plans the minute particulars of earning one's livelihood in its many aspects—and that is generally outside all of the stages of trust in God. Yet everyone can be found in this degree; I mean, seeking to acquire by effort subtle ways of attaining, in a permissible manner, wealth that is permitted. But to acquire something that is legally questionable, or to seek to acquire something in such a manner, represents the outer limit of coveting what is worldly and of trusting in means. It is hardly a secret that this renders trust in God nugatory, and is like having recourse to certain kinds of means to gain something beneficial, as when one turns to charms, [the entrails of] birds, or branding as a way of removing harm. The Prophet ﷺ described all this to those who trust in God, and he did not tell them that such people were not engaged in earning a livelihood or living in cities or acquiring things; he was rather remarking to them that such people occupied themselves with this sort of means. Means like this, which people trust will attain certain results, are too numerous to count.

Sahl considered that trust in divine providence meant renouncing planning, so he said: "God created human beings without hiding them from Himself, but they are hidden by their planning."[31] Perhaps he was referring to those who contrive means so unlikely that thinking about them requires that one's planning proceed outside manifest means. Thus it should be clear that means are divided into those which draw us away from trust in divine providence when we depend upon them, and those which do not. Further, those which do not draw one away are divided into sure and apparent [means]. Those which are sure do not draw one away from such trust with respect to the existence of the state of trust in God and the knowledge connected with it. For this involves trusting in the cause of the means, and trust in God in this degree consists in the state and in knowledge, but not in actions. When it comes to apparent means, trust in God in this degree consists in the state and in knowledge, yet in actions as well. Moreover, those who trust in God in connection with these means may be considered on three different levels.

The first is the station of [Ibrahim] al-Hawwās and those like him: he is the one who wandered in the desert without provisions, confident in the favor of God Most High towards him, to strengthen him to endure a week or even more, to let there be grass or other nourishment for him—or let him be confirmed in complete approval [*riḍā'*] regarding death if none of these eventuate. For whoever carries provisions may also lose them or his mount may go astray and he could die of hunger—this is possible to one with provisions just as it is possible to someone deprived of them. The second station belongs to one who sits in his house or in a mosque, yet in a village or town. This level is lower than the first, though [285] he is also one who trusts in God because he renounces gaining a livelihood and visible means, relying on the favor of God Most High in planning things by way of hidden means, and eschews means of sustenance by remaining seated in the town. Yet while gaining a livelihood entails using means, it need not nullify one's trust in God, since one's gaze can be directed to the very One who keeps the one who remains in place in servitude to Himself. Yet this one's sustenance is connected with what he does, while it is not so for the one who remains in his place, since one could imagine the rest of the people overlooking and neglecting him, were it not for the grace of God Most High motivating them and confirming their resolve.

The third level consists in going out and gaining one's livelihood in the manner which we have already noted in chapters three and four of the Book on the Ethics of Earning a Livelihood [of the *Iḥyā'*], nor need that pursuit either remove one from the stations of trust in God, so long as one's peace of soul does not rest on self-sufficiency or self-confidence, on one's position or one's wealth—for it could be that God Most High would destroy all that in a moment. Rather is his gaze fixed on the authentic trustee, to safeguard all those things and to facilitate means for him, since he sees his livelihood, his wealth, and his sufficiency in vital connection with the omnipotence of God Most High, as he saw the pen fixed in the hand of the king. His gaze was not fixed on the pen but on the heart of the king by which it was set in motion, inclined, and directed. For if such a one gains livelihood for his family or to distribute it to the poor, his body is indeed provided for, but his heart quite separated from it, and this state is superior to that state of one who remains seated in his house.

The proof that earning a livelihood need not nullify the state of trust in God—so long as one keeps the conditions in mind and connects it with the state [*tawakkul*] and the knowledge [*tawḥīd*]—comes from the righteous one [*as-Siddiq*—Abū Bakr]. When he was acclaimed caliph he went out one morning carrying clothes under his arm and a measuring rod in his hand, and entered the market to hawk them. The Muslims were disgusted with him, and said: "How can you do that when you just assumed the role of caliph of the Prophet ﷺ [i.e., the one who takes his place]?" And he responded: "Do not alienate me from my family, for if I neglect them, whom might I neglect after them?" So they saw to it that the members of the family received food from the Muslim community, and once they agreed to that and he saw that it made them happy and pleased their hearts, he occupied his time with the well-being of Muslims first of all.[32] Now it is impossible to say that the righteous one [Abū Bakr] is not at the station of trust in God! Indeed, who would come before him in this station? For the proof that he is one who trusts in God does not proceed from a perspective of renouncing pursuit of livelihood but from that of cutting off any inclination towards his sustenance and sufficiency, and the knowledge that God Himself will facilitate a livelihood, organize the means, and keep the conditions in mind in the way of making one's livelihood. Such a one will be satisfied with what he needs, without asking for more, boasting or hoarding, or preferring his own dirhams to those of others. For whoever enters the market preferring his own dirhams to those of others is intent on this world and in love with it.[33] And trust in God cannot flourish without some renunciation [*zuhd*] of this world, though renunciation may flourish without such trust, for trust in divine providence is a station beyond that of renunciation.

Abū Ja'far al-Ḥaddād, the sheikh of al-Junayd—may God be generous to both of them—who was one of those who trust in God, said: "I have kept trust in God hidden for twenty years, and not kept away from the market. I earned a dinar each day, but did not keep a danīq of it overnight, nor did I enjoy even a qīrāt to go into the bath, but I gave it away before nightfall." And al-Junayd would not speak of trust in God in his presence, but rather said: "I cannot speak of that station when he is here with me."[34] You should know that remaining in a Sufi convent with an assured support is far from trust in God, for even if there is no assured support or endowment, yet the servants are ordered to go out and beg, that cannot rightly be called trust in God, except in an attenuated sense. Nonetheless, it can be supplemented by [the appropriate] state and knowledge, as with the trust in God of one who earns his livelihood. But as for those who do not ask but simply take what is brought to them, their trust in God is enhanced in that regard, though their situation is better known than those in the market. And that is the case for anyone who goes into the market, for as we have noted, one cannot go into the market as one who trusts in God without [having fulfilled] many conditions.

You might ask whether it is better to sit in one's house or to go out to earn one's livelihood? You should know that one may be freed to renounce earning one's livelihood for reflection [*fikr*] or remembrace [*dhikr*], or for sincere devotion and to dedicate time to prayer, since earning one's way can disturb one from such things. And when one is more occupied with them, and does not look up to people expecting them to come to him and bring him anything, but is rather strong of heart in steadfastness and trust in God Most High, renunciation is better for him. But for one whose heart is agitated at home and looks up to people, it is better that he earn his living, for the heart's looking up to people is the heart's way of petitioning, and it is more important to renounce that than to renounce earning one's living. For those who trust in God are not intent on getting what their souls look up to.[35] Aḥmad b. Ḥanbal once asked Abū Bakr al-Marwazī to give a certain poor person some of the compensation for which he had contracted with him. When the man in question turned away, and even while he was turning around, Aḥmad told [al-Marwazī]: "Catch up with him and give it to him; he will receive it." So he caught up with him, gave it to him, and he took it; [286] and when [al-Marwazī] asked Aḥmad about it, he said: "His soul had been looking for this above all, and he had gone out for that very reason. But once his hope was blocked, he despaired, so he took it."[36] And when [Ibrahim] al-Hawwās—may God's mercy be upon him—saw that someone was in his gift, or feared that his soul could become habituated to that, he would take nothing from him.[37] Having been asked what marvels he had seen in his travels, al-Hawwās said: "I saw al-Kadir, and he was pleased to accompany me, but I distanced myself from him for fear that my soul would rest in him and be diminished in trust in God."[38] So one who earns his livelihood, so long as he observes the ethics of earning with its condition (as we noted in the Book of Ethics [of Earning a Livelihood]), and does not aim at acquiring more nor put his reliance in his wealth or his sufficiency, can also be one who trusts in divine providence.

But you might ask: How can we know that someone is not placing his trust in wealth or sufficiency? I would say that we can know by his reaction if his wealth is stolen or his business fails, or any of his affairs are impeded. Is he content with that? Is his peace [of soul] intact and his heart not agitated? Even more, was the state of his heart equally at peace before and after the event? For if a person does not rely on anything, he will not be agitated to lose it; and if one is agitated at losing something, he has indeed relied on it. Al-Bishr worked a spindle and gave it up as a result of al-Baᶜādi writing to him: "I heard that you have come upon hard times sustaining yourself with a spindle. Where do you think sustenance will come from if God takes away your hearing and your sight?" That struck his heart, and he removed the tool of the spindle from his hand and gave it up.[39] It is said that he gave it up because [his work] was acclaimed with his name, and he was sought after because of it. It is also said that he did it when his family had died, like the fifty dinars which Sufyān [aṭ-Ṭawrī] had for doing business, which he distributed when his family died.[40]

Yet you may ask: How is it conceivable that one have wealth and does not rely on it, since he knows that earning without wealth is impossible? I would answer: since he knows many to whom God Most High gives sustenance, and many others whose great wealth has been stolen or wiped out. And he may also reconcile himself to the fact that God only does with him what is best for him: that if his wealth be wiped out, that is better for him, since perhaps if it were left to him it would have become a factor corrupting his religion, so that God Most High had in fact been gracious to him. The worst case would be his dying of hunger, but it is enough that he be convinced that death from hunger is better for him in the next world, in the measure that God Most High decided that for him, and it was not a result of any defect on his part. Once he is convinced of all of that, the presence or absence of wealth is all the same to him. As a tradition says: "A man proposed one evening to undertake a business venture which, had he carried it out would have meant his destruction, but God Most High looked down on him from His throne and kept him from it. In the morning he was dejected and sad, and saw an evil omen in his neighbor and cousin: 'Who got there before me? Who outsmarted me?' But what was that but a mercy which God mercifully bestowed on him?"[41]

ᶜUmar—may God be pleased with him—spoke of this as well: "It matters not to me whether I happen to be rich or poor, for I cannot tell which of the two would be better for me." Now whoever cannot attain perfect certainty regarding these matters cannot conceivably become one who trusts in God. Abū Sulaymān ad-Dārānī spoke about that [to his disciple] Aḥmad b. Abī'l-Hawārī: "I have a place on every station, except for this blessed trust in divine providence; I have not even sniffed a whiff of it."[42] He said this despite the greatness of his power, nor did he mention its being among the attainable states, but he rather said: "I have not reached it." Perhaps he had an even higher awareness in mind. So long as one lacks perfect faith that there is no agent but God and no sustainer other than He, or that everything which He arranges for human beings is best for them, whether poverty or riches, death or life, and so finds himself at peace—[until that happens] the state of trust in divine providence is not yet perfect. For such trust is grounded in the intensity of faith in such matters, as we have already indicated, just as similar stations of religion, with the saying and deeds proper to them, are built on the foundation of faith. Put succinctly, trust in divine providence is a state that can be understood, but it requires a strong heart and intense certainty [*yaqīn*]. So it was that Sahl said: "Whoever discredits gaining a livelihood has discredited divine practice [*sunna*], and whoever discredits giving up gaining a livelihood has discredited faith in divine unity."[43] [287]

You might ask: Is there a therapy one might utilize to keep the heart from relying on visible means and to think favorably of the way God Most High puts hidden means at one's disposal? I say to that: indeed! What you must learn is that unfavorable thoughts [about God] are insinuations of Satan, while fitting ones are the inspiration of God Most High, as He says: "Satan threatens you with poverty and constrains you to foul ways. God's promise to you is of His forgiveness and generosity" [2:268]. By his nature man is fascinated by listening to the insinuations of Satan, so it is said: "One who is apprehensive is one intent on evil thoughts."[44] And when cowardice and a weak heart are joined to them, and one considers those who put their trust in visible means and are motivated by them, then evil thoughts will take over, and for the most part, trust in God is overcome. But stories of sustenance by hidden means can also overcome trust in divine providence. The story is told of a man who had sequestered himself in a mosque, and had no determinate means of support, so the imam told him that it would be better for him to earn a living. He did not answer him until he had repeated it three times, but on the fourth time he said: "A Jew in the vicinity of the mosque assured me of two flat loaves of bread each day." The imam said: "If he was just in his assurance, then staying here in the mosque is better for you." To which the man responded: "You there! If you were not an imam, confident before God and before man despite such lack of faith in divine unity, it would be better for you [to earn your living], for you have given a Jew's word preference over the assurance of God Most High to give sustenance."[45] An imam of a mosque said to a Muslim: "Whence do you eat?" He responded, "O sheikh, wait until the celebration of prayer, which I shall pray standing behind you; then I will answer you."[46]

It helps to think well of the way in which sustenance from God Most High comes from hidden means to listen to the stories which tell of the wonderful things God had done to bring sustenance to those who belong to Him, as well as the wonders of God's dominating by destroying the possessions of businessmen and rich persons; even to letting them die of hunger. So it was said of Ḥudhayfa [b. Qatāda] al-Marashī, who was the servant of Ibrāhīm b. Adham, that when he was asked what marvels he had seen happen to Ibrāhīm, he answered: "We had been enroute to Mecca for days and had not found anything to eat, when we came to Kufa and took refuge in the ruins of a mosque. Ibrāhīm looked at me and said: 'O Ḥudhayfa, I see hunger in you'. I responded: 'That is indeed what the sheikh sees'! So he said: 'Bring me an inkwell and paper'. I brought these to him and he wrote: 'In the name of God the Infinitely Good, the Merciful: You are the One who intends all states and is aware of all meanings'. Then he wrote this poem:

I am one who praises, who thanks, who remembers,
Who is hungry, scrawny, and naked.
They are six and I am assured half of them.
O Creator, assure me half of them.
My praise for others is a blazing fire striking terror in them;
Keep your servants from entering the fire.

Then he handed me the piece of paper, saying: 'Go out and do not let your heart depend on anything but God Most High. Hand the piece of paper to the first one whom you meet'. So I went out and the first person whom I met was a man on a mule. I held the paper out to him and he took it. When he had read what it said he asked: 'What does he do—the one whose paper this is'? I said: 'He is in such and such a mosque', and he handed me a purse with 600 dinars. Then I met another man and asked him about the one riding a mule. He said: 'He is a Christian'. So I came back to Ibrāhīm and told him the story, whereupon he said: 'Do not touch the purse, for the man will be coming presently'. After a bit the Christian came in, bowed to Ibrāhīm's head, kissed it, and embraced Islam!"[47]

Abu Ya'qūb al-Aqṭa' al-Baṣrī said: "Once I undertook a voluntary fast for ten days in the holy sanctuary [of Mecca], and I became weak. My soul told me to go out, so I went out into the square perchance to find something to ameliorate my weakness. I saw a turnip that had been thrown away, and I picked it up. Yet my heart felt forlorn when I did that, as if someone were speaking to me and saying: 'You have fasted for ten days, and after that it is your good fortune to find a rotten turnip!' So I threw it away and entered the mosque [288] and sat down. Then a man who was not Arab approached, sat down before me, put down a satchel and said: 'This is for you'. When I asked him how it could be that this was especially for me, he answered: 'Know that I was at sea for ten days and the ship was on the verge of capsizing when I vowed that, if God Most High would save me, I would give this as alms to the first one I should happen to see in the vicinity of the sanctuary. You are the first whom I met'. So I said: 'Open it', and he opened it and there was Egyptian baked bread, distinctive almonds, and sugar cubes. So I took a handful of this and a handful of that, and said: 'take the rest to your family as a gift from me to all of you, for I have received it'. Then I said to myself: 'He sustained you, facilitating [your fast] for ten days, and you sought sustenance in the gutter'!"[48]

Mamshāḍ al-Dīnawarī said: "I had a debt against me, and my heart was absorbed with its implications, and in a dream it seemed as if someone were speaking and said: 'You miser! Take from us the amount of the debt. Take it! Taking belongs to you and giving to us.' After that I contracted no more obligations—neither with greengrocers, butchers, or anyone else!"[49] One tells of Bunān al-Ḥammāl that he said: "I was on the road to Mecca coming from Egypt, and I had provisions with me. A woman came up to me and said to me: 'O Bunān, you are a porter, carrying provision on your back. Do you suppose He will not give you sustenance?' Once she spoke I threw away my provisions. After three days had passed and I had not eaten, I found a footring in the road, and said to myself: 'I will wear it until its owner comes, and perhaps he will give me something when I give it back to him'. Then that woman was there again and she said to me: 'You are a merchant who says: its owner will come and give me something for it'. Then she threw me some dirhams and said: 'Give it away'. With that I was happy to be near Mecca!" It is told of Bunān that he needed a maidservant to take care of him. So he let his brother know this, and his brother got enough money together for him to purchase her, and said to him:

"Here it is. The group is coming; let it buy what suits you." When the entire party arrived, they saw one and said: "That one looks good for him, and said to her master: "How much is that one?" To which he responded: "She is not for sale." When they pressed him, he said: "She belongs to Bunān al-Hammāl. A woman from Samarkand gave her to him as a present, and sent her to Bunān, so you should take her to him and tell him the story."[50]

It is said that once upon a time there was a man on a journey who had a loaf of bread with him. He said: "Once I eat this I shall be dead." God—Great and Glorious—entrusted him to an angel and said: "If he eats it, give him sustenance; but if he does not eat it, do not give him anything." And the loaf stayed with him without his eating it, until he died; so the loaf of bread outlasted him." Abū Sa'īd al-Kharrāz said: "I had entered the desert with no provisions, and when need overcame me and I saw a waystation from afar, I rejoiced that I would soon arrive there, and then reflected to myself that I was at peace and trusting in none other than Him, so I swore not to enter the waystation unless someone brought me to it. So I dug a hole in the sand and hid my body in it until sunrise. But I heard a loud shout at midnight: 'O people of the waystation! There is a friend of God Most High who has imprisoned himself in the sand. Go get him!' So all of them came and took me out and carried me to the place."[51] It is related that a man remained standing by the door of ʿUmar—may God be pleased with him—who finally said to him: "You there! Are you coming here to ʿUmar or to God Most High? Go and learn the Qur'an so that you will not need [to stand by] the door of ʿUmar." So the man left and stayed away until ʿUmar missed him; in fact he kept away and devoted himself to prayer. Then ʿUmar came and said to him: "Even if I separated myself from you, what alienated you from me?" He said: "I have recited the Qur'an and it made ʿUmar and ʿUmar's family quite unnecessary to me." ʿUmar responded: "May God be merciful to you for what you found there;"

so he recited what he found there: "'In the heavens I will give you sustenance and what was promised you'[51:22], saying: 'my sustenance was in heaven while I sought it on earth'!" ʿUmar wept and said: "You are blessed," and after that ʿUmar looked upon him with favor and sat with him.[52] [289]

Abū Hamza al-Khurāsānī reported: "I was making the hajj one of the two years [in which I made it], and I was walking along the road when I fell into a well, and my soul struggled with me whether to cry for help. But I said: 'No, by God! I shall not cry for help'. I had not completed this thought when two men appeared at the top of the well, and one cried to the other at the top of his voice: 'Let us cover this open well lest someone fall into it'. They brought reeds and a mat and covered the opening of the well. I was on the point of screaming when I said to myself: 'The One to whom I will scream is closer than these two', and I put myself at rest. Indeed in less than an hour someone came and uncovered the well and put his foot into it, saying to me: 'Hang onto me' with a growl. When I understood what he was saying, I hung onto him and he pulled me out, for he was a lion. Then a voice called out to me: ʿAbu Hamza, is this not better? We have used a destructive thing to keep you from destruction.' So I responded by saying:

My diffidence keeps me from unveiling my desire,
Yet You have substituted for that unveiling a
knowledge of Yourself.
You have dealt kindly with my affairs and clarified
my sight
Into my hidden recesses, where grace is attained
by grace.
You look through me into my hidden recesses; it is
as though
You touch me there and you are in the palm of my hand.

I see you and within me my viscera recoil in dread
of You,
Yet you befriend me with Your grace and Your
loving care.
You keep the beloved alive with love for his death,
Hence the marvel of life being yoked together
with death."[53]

Incidents like this abound, and when faith is intensified by them and is joined by the power to endure hunger for the space of a week with no crimping of the heart; or when faith is so intensified that should sustenance not come to him in a week, then death is better for him in the eyes of God—Great and Glorious—and that is how he counts on Him; then is trust in divine providence perfected through these states and visions. Indeed, it cannnot be perfected in any other way.

[3.12.] *Explaining the trust in divine providence proper to heads of families*

You should know that the judgment of one responsible for a family must differ from that of a single person. For single persons can only be said to have an authentic trust in divine providence when two things are present. The first is the capacity to endure hunger for a week without looking around [for help] nor letting the spirit be crimped; while the second regards forms of faith as we have explained them: that he would willingly accept death if no one gave him sustenance, conscious that his sustenance lay in hunger and death, since whatever was denied him in this world would be recovered in the next. So he sees that two better forms of sustenance have come to him: one is sustenance in the next world, and the other the illness which visits him with death, yet with which he can be content as with something decided and destined for him. In this way is trust in divine providence perfected in the single person.

But it is not permissible that one who provides for a household be charged with enduring hunger, nor can that faith in divine unity be required of them in which death from hunger is the sustenance of one whose soul is blessed—even though such a thing would rarely happen; so there must be other forms of faith. In fact, no other trust in divine providence is possible for them than that available to one who earns his livelihood, where the third station of trust in God is like that of Abū Bakr, the righteous one—may God be pleased with him—who went out to earn his livelihood. But so far as going into the desert or leaving one's family, a trust of that sort is not for them; and the same for a trust in God which would keep them from concern for their affairs—all this is prohibited them. For it could result in their ruin and in fact be blameworthy for them, since the truth of the matter is that there is no difference between them and their families. By that same token, however, if the family were to favor enduring hunger for a while or even trust in death from hunger as their sustenance and a benefit in the next world, both he and they would be trusting in divine providence.

Similarly, a man's soul is a family to him, so it is not permissible for him to neglect it unless it be in favor of enduring hunger for a while. But if it cannot endure it, or if his heart would be in turmoil or his worship upset by such a practice, he is not permitted to trust in that way. The story of Abū Turāb an-Nakhshabī is relevant here. He oncc watched a Sufi pick up a melon rind to eat it after three days, and said to him: "Sufism is hardly beneficial for you; you had better go into the market."[54] That is to say: there is no sufism without trust in divine providence, and there is no authentic trust in God unless one can refrain from food for more than three days. So Abū ʿAlī ar-Rudhabarī said: "If a poor man says after five days 'I am hungry' he should go to the market and begin to work and earn his livelihood."[55] Moreover, a man's body is family to him, so that his trust in God with respect to harming his body is like his trust in

God with regard to his family, even though they differ in one respect: that one may charge oneself with enduring hunger, but not one's family.

Now it has already been unveiled to you [290] from all this that trust in divine providence does not consist in cutting oneself off from means, but rather is grounded in enduring hunger for a while, and in being content with death in the rare chance that sustenance arrive too late. Depending on a nation or a city, or depending on a desert which is not bereft of grass—all such things are means of survival, and so not without a certain sort of harm, hence it is impossible to be sustained by them without patience. So trusting in divine providence in cities is very close to the forms of trust in the desert. All of these are means, yet people make use of means manifest to them without considering them to be means, due to the weakness of their faith and the strength of their desire. They also have little or no capacity to sustain the trials of this world for the sake of the next, for fear has mastered their hearts as thinking is corrupted and hope recedes indefinitely.

Whoever contemplates the intelligible world [*malakūt*] of the heavens and the earth has in effect had unveiled to them that God Most High has arranged this world and the intelligible world [*malakūt*] in an orderly fashion so that human beings will not lose their sustenance if they let go of their busyness, nor would they lose their sustenance if they were unable to busy themselves. Consider the fetus within its mother: it is unable to busy itself yet its navel is connected with the mother so that an abundance of nourishment comes to it from her by means of the umbilical cord, yet in no wise does that reflect any deliberation on the part of the fetus. And once it has been separated from its mother, love and compassion take over in the mother to assume responsibility for [the infant]—whether she wants to or not, for she is constrained by God Most High to undertake her responsibilities in the measure that the fire of love is kindled in her heart. Then, since the infant has no teeth with which to chew food, he receives his sustenance from milk which needs no mastication, and given the softness of his physical constitution, one cannot give him solid food, so He makes abundant milk flow to him from the breasts of his mother until he detaches himself from them when he senses he has had enough. Now does all this happen by deliberation of the infant or of the mother? When it is appropriate that he take solid food, he will sprout teeth—incisors and eye-teeth—for chewing. And when he grows up and becomes independent, means are available to him to learn to pursue the paths which lead to the next life.[56]

So it is consummate ignorance to be anxious once one reaches maturity, for the means of livelihood do not diminish once one reaches maturity, but they rather increase. And although one is not yet able to earn a livelihood, one is nearly able to do so for one's power is increasing, and at least one person has compassion for him—his mother or father. Moreover, their compassion is overflowing, for they give him food and drink twice a day, and their feeding him comes about as a result of God Most High bringing love and compassion to bear on their hearts. Furthermore, God has also brought compassion, love, mercy, and gentleness to bear on the hearts of Muslims—indeed in all those resident in the land—to the point where each one of them, when they notice someone in need, will be moved in their heart to give him sustenance, and a motivation [*dāʿī*] will be incited in them to eliminate his need. While there had been one who had compassion on him, now there are a thousand or more; moreover, no one had been showing compassion towards him because they saw him in the care of his mother or father, where he was their special object of compassion when they noticed him needing something. Yet were anyone to notice that he was an orphan, God would bring to bear on a Muslim or on the community the motivation to take him and care for him. For we have not heard up to the present time of an orphan dying of hunger in times of abundance, even though he be unable to busy himself and lack a special protector, for God Most High is his protector by means of the compassion which he creates in the hearts of human beings.

So why should it be necessary that one's heart be taken up with finding sustenance after one reaches maturity while it was not so occupied during childhood, when there had been one showing compassion towards him then while there are now a thousand? To be sure, his mother's compassion was more intense and more gracious, yet she was but one person; and while the compassion of any one of the people may be weak, what results from all of them together certainly serves one's needs—indeed, how many are the orphans whose situation God Most High has made easy, and in fact better than the situation of those who have a father or mother. For He has made up for the weak compassion of one person by many who showed compassion, and by removing luxury and restricting hardship to what one can bear. What the poet has said about this is quite beautiful:

> The pen of the judge related how things are:
> That activity and tranquillity are on equal terms.
> It is madness for you to seek your sustenance
> When the fetus is given sustenance in its shell.

But you will say: people care for the orphan because they see that he is helpless, being a child, but once this one has reached maturity he is then able to earn his livelihood, so they will not attend to him but will rather say: "he is like us; let him do something for himself." I would answer that if all he can do is be idle, they are right; he should earn his livelihood, and it makes no sense to speak of trust in divine providence in his case. For trust in divine providence is one of the states of religion which one uses to be free for God Most High, and what can being idle have to do with trusting in God? But if he is devoted to God, remaining in the mosque or at home, and assiduous in learning and in prayer, people will not blame him for renouncing earning a livelihood, nor will they begrudge him that. Quite the contrary, his devotion to God Most High confirms [291] the hearts of the people in their love for him, so that they bring him more than he needs. As for himself, he best not close his door or flee from people to the mountains, for to this day one has never seen a learned or prayerful man who lived in the city and devoted his time to God Most High die of hunger. On the other hand, if He wanted to feed all of the people with His word, He could do so. For if anyone devotes himself to God Most High, God Great and Glorious will devote Himself to him; so that if anyone is devoted to God—Great and Glorious— God will put love for him into the hearts of the people so that their hearts will serve him as the heart of a mother serves her child. For God Most High arranged this world and the intelligible world in an orderly fashion sufficient for the people of these worlds, and whoever sees this order trusts in the One who so orders it, and devotes himself to Him, putting his faith in and contemplating the One who orders the means rather than in the means themselves.

To be sure, He has not so arranged that those devoted to Him enjoy a life of unremitting sweetness, succulent birds, fine clothes, or high-spirited horses—not at all; even though that may happen in certain situations. Rather has He so ordered things that everyone devoted to the worship of God Most High may be assured that each week a loaf of barley bread or some greens will be supplied to them without fail. And most of the time they will receive more than that, exceeding the extent of what they need or what would suffice, so there is no reason for forsaking trust in God unless it be the soul's lusting for unremitting luxuries: tunics of luxuriant cloth or a supply of gourmet food—and none of that spells a way to the next world. Nor can anything like that be expected without a great deal of work, and with rare exceptions not even a great deal of work will secure it; though in rare cases it may even be attained without any work! So the [importance of] the fruits of such work diminish once one's inner vision is opened, and as a result one cannot find rest in one's own efforts, but rather in the One who arranges this world and the intelligible world in an ordered way so that none of his servants is overlooked when it comes to sustenance, even should he remain at home—except for the exceedingly rare situation when something similar may be conceived with regard to one who works by his own efforts.

When these matters are unveiled so that strength comes into the heart and courage into the soul, what results has been expressed by Ḥasan al-Baṣrī—may God be merciful to him—when he said: "Would that everyone in Basra belonged to my family, and compassion could be had for a dinar!"[57] And Wuhayb b. al-Ward [al-Makkī] said: "If heaven were made of copper and earth of lead, and I were determined to seek my sustenance, I would become an unbeliever."[58] Once you have understood these things, you will have understood that trust in divine providence is one station among the stations of the soul, and that it is possible for one who has mastered his soul to attain it. You will also know that one may reject the very principle of such trust and that it is possible to reject it out of ignorance. But beware of confusing two sorts of failure: failing to have any taste [*dhawq*] for this station, and failing to believe in it—more a failure of knowledge. Once you are content with very little and satisfied with your sustenance, it will doubtless be given to you, even if you flee from it.[59] Accordingly it belongs to God to restore your sustenance to you by the hand of someone whom you do not count on. If you prepare yourself by fear of God as well as trust in Him, you will see by experience the confirmation of what the Most High says: *Whoever truly fears God, He will make for him a way through and provide for him from sources he never envisaged* [65:2-3]. What a marvel! Yet he did not assure him that he would feed him meat of birds or sweetmeats from the table; what He guaranteed was a sustenance which would sustain his life. Yet this guarantee is shared by all who devote themselves to the One who guarantees it and who trusts in His guarantee. And should someone become completely familiar with the way in which God orders the hidden means of sustenance, he will stand out among those who contemplate creation. For the conduits of sustenance cannot be counted and the channels which carry it are not to be discovered, since whatever may be visible on earth has its cause in heaven. God Most High says: *In the heavens is your provision and all that you are pledged* [51:22], yet the hidden places of the heavens do not show themselves to us.

A group came to see al-Junayd regarding this topic, and he said to them: "What are you looking for?" they answered: "We are looking for sustenance." So he said: "If you know where He is sitting, ask Him." They said: "Should we ask God?" He retorted: "If you know that He has forgotten you, then remember Him." They said: "We shall return home, trust in God, and see what happens." But he answered: "Trusting in God as a kind of experiment is a form of doubt." They said: "What strategy have we?" To which he replied: "Renounce any strategy!"[60] [Abū Sa'īd] Aḥmad b. ʿIsā al-Kharrāz said: "I was in the desert when a terrible hunger came upon me, so I prevailed upon my soul to ask God Most High for food. Then I said: 'This is not what those who trust in God would do'. So [my soul] demanded that I ask God for patience. When I set myself to do that I heard an invisible voice call to me, saying:

He declares that He is close to us
    And we must not lose what has been given us.
He invites us to choose force
    As though we do not see Him nor He us."[292]

Now you have already understood that for anyone whose soul has been tamed[61] and his heart strengthened, whose inner resolve has not been weakened by anxiety and whose faith in the order of God Most High has been intensified: his soul is continually at rest as he hopes in God—Great and Glorious. His state is the same as that of a corpse, and death will no doubt come to him just as it comes to one whose soul is not at rest, so trust in God is made perfect from our side by perfect contentment [*riḍā'*] and from God's by fulfilling what He has guaranteed. For He is the One who guarantees sustenance to all who are content by those means which He arranges in a just fashion. So rest content, and confirm by seeing for yourself the justice of the promise realizing what He intends for you by way of sustenance: wonders which are beyond your imagining or reckoning. Let it not be part of your trust in God to have any expectations of means but rather of the One who causes means to be means, just as you do not expect anything from the pen of the writer but from his heart as the source of the movement of the pen; and the first mover is One, so it is not necessary that you look to anyone other than to Him.

This is the condition for trusting in God proper to anyone who plunges into the desert without provisions or for someone undistinguished who remains in the city. But for one who is known for his prayer or knowledge, if he is content with food once in the space of a day or a night, this is how it will be: there will not be delicacies but rough garments as befits a man of religion, yet that will come to him, whether he thinks about it or not, in perpetuity. He will even be given more in addition. Yet such a one has left trust in God behind, as well as any concern for sustenance, to an extreme limit of weakness and diminishment. If he is well-known, for obvious reasons the sustenance that will come to him will be greater than that [coming] to one who enters the city as someone unknown or who earns his livelihood. Concern for sustenance is repugnant to a person of religion, and even more so if he be among those learned in religious matters, for contentment is a condition of their life. And the learned among them are content that they will receive their sustenance, which taken together in fact amounts to a great deal. If it should be that they receive nothing from the community, then He does not want them to take from the hands of people but to eat from their own livelihood; indeed that is the way suitable to intellectuals who journey to Him by way of exoteric knowledge and effort, but do not participate in an inner journey. Earning a livelihood is not permitted on the path of interior poverty *[fiqr]*, where one is expected to devote oneself to the journey while receiving what is given to them from the hands of those who seek the favor of God Most High first, that they might be free for God—Great and Glorious, and also to help to those who give to them attain their reward. Whoever contemplates the course of the ways [*sunna*] of God Most High knows that sustenance is never in proportion to means. One may illustrate that by the question one of the Persian kings put to a wise man about a fool prospering while an intelligent person suffered privation. He was told: "The creator intended to demonstrate something of Himself in this. For had He given sustenance to every intelligent person and left fools deprived, one might think that intelligence gives sustenance to those who possess it; but when they see that the opposite holds true, they know that the One who sustains is not one of them, and they will not put their confidence in visible means." As the poet says:

> Were sustenance to proceed according to wit,
> Animals would perish from ignorance.

[3.13.] *Using a parable to clarify the states of those who trust in God while depending on means*

Take this parable of a group of beggars gathered in the square before the gate of the king's palace and let it serve as an allegory for the relation of creatures to God Most High. They were in need of food and the king sent many servants out to them with loaves of bread, ordering them to give some two loaves and others one, making every effort not to overlook a single one of them. He ordered the crier to announce to them: "Be quiet and don't grab hold of my servants when they come out to you. Each of you should remain calm in his place, for the servants are subservient to me and they have their orders to give you your food. When the doors to the square are opened and they come out, should anyone grab hold of the servants to harm them and take two loaves, I will pursue him with a servant to take charge of him until I am ready to punish him, at a time known to me and concealed from him. But for those who do not harm the servants, are content with the single loaf given them by the hand of a servant, and keep quiet, I shall confer on them a brilliant robe of honor at the appointed time in place of the punishment the others received. And whoever remains in his place but takes two loaves will neither be punished nor receive a robe of honor. Should there be anyone whom my servants overlook and hence do not give anything, provided he spends the night hungry without exasperating the servants or complaining 'if only he had given me a loaf', when morning comes I will make him a minister and entrust my kingdom to him."

The beggars soon divided into four groups. One group consisted of those whose stomachs prevailed over them and they did not heed the warnings about punishments; instead they said: "From today to the morrow is a long time, and we are hungry now!" So they fell upon the servants, harming them and taking two loaves. Punishment befell them at the time mentioned; they regretted what they had done but their remorse was of no avail. Another group kept from taking hold of the servants for fear of punishment, but took two loaves out of the hunger which mastered them. They escaped punishment but did not win a robe of honor. A third group said: "Let us gather in view of the servants so they do not overlook us, and if they give us [293] one loaf, let us take it and be content with it, and it may be that we win a robe of honor"—which they did. A fourth group hid themselves in a corner of the square out of sight of the servants, saying: "If they pursue us and give something to us we shall be content with one loaf, but should they overlook us we shall endure the hardship of hunger all night long. Perhaps we will be strong enough to keep from exasperation so that we will gain the rank of minister and a level of proximity to the king." But that did not profit them, since the servants pursued them in every corner and gave each of them one loaf. Things went on like that for days, until it happened by chance that three of them hid in a corner and the servants did not chance to spy them, preoccupied as they were and so diverted from an extensive search. So they spent the night in a terrible hunger, and two of them said: "If only we had made ourselves known to the servants and taken our food, for we cannot endure any longer!" The third, however, remained still until morning and attained the level of proximity as well as the status of minister.

This is an allegory of creation: the square is life in this world, the gate opening onto the square is death, the unknown time is the day of resurrection. The promise of becoming minister is the promise of vision offered to those who trust in divine providence that should they die of hunger they may be content that there will be no delay in the time of resurrection—since martyrs are alive: "With their Lord they have their sustenance" [3:169]. Those who laid hold of the servants are those who rely on means, while the servants subservient to them are the means. Those who gathered in the square in full sight of the servants are those who remain in convents and mosques in a state of tranquillity, while those hidden in a corner are those who wander in the desert in a state of trust in God, while the means pursue them and sustenance is given them—and this happens not infrequently. Should one of them die from hunger, he will be content, for he will be a martyr and enjoy proximity to God Most High. So creatures are divided into these four groups, and it may be that out of every hundred [persons], ninety will depend on means, while seven of the remaining ten will stay in the city [and succeed in] resisting having recourse to means by their sheer presence and reputation.

Three will wander in the desert, two of whom will become exasperated while one will attain to proximity. Perhaps it was like that in times gone by; but today those who renounce means do not reach to one in ten thousand.

[3.2.] *Attending to means by saving*

Whoever obtains wealth for himself by inheritance, endeavor, asking, or utilizing means can adopt [one of] three attitudes towards saving. First, one takes what one needs for the moment, eats when one is hungry, dresses when one is naked, purchases a small house when he needs it, and distributes the rest immediately. He takes and saves only what he perceives that he deserves or needs, so his saving will follow this pattern as well—all that accords with an authentic trust in divine providence and so constitutes the highest degree. The second attitude is the opposite of this and removes one from the domain of trust in God: such a one stores up for a year or more, and this has nothing at all to do with trusting in God. Indeed it is said: "only three kinds of animals store things up: mice, ants, and children of Adam." The third attitude is of one who stores up for forty days or less. As for this one, must he be kept from the place of praise in the next world promised to those who trust in God? Authorities differ on this: Sahl is of the opinion that such a one is outside the limits of trust in God, but [Ibrahīm] al-Khawāṣṣ teaches that a period forty days does not put one outside such trust while more than forty days would; while Abū Ṭālib al Makkī says that even more than forty days will not put one beyond trust in God.[62]

Such a controversy makes no sense once the principle of saving has been permitted. Of course one may have one's own thoughts whether the very principle of saving is not contrary to trust in God, yet to discriminate among people afterwards would not be reasonable at all. For all recompense promised to a rank is distributed throughout the rank, and each rank has an initial and a final stage. Those who have attained the final stage are "those who are foremost" [56:10], while those who have reached the first are said to be "those on the right hand" [56:27]. Now these last have attained the rank as well as "those who are foremost," and the highest levels of "those on the right hand" are contiguous with the lowest levels of "those who are foremost," so it makes no sense at all to discriminate among these grades. On the contrary, one can in fact only attain that trust in God which renounces saving when one's expectations are limited. For no one in his right mind looks forward to living a long time while removing the very conditions for such life, for that would be quite impossible to bring about. People differ in the span of their expectation—whether longer or shorter, the shortest degree of expectation is a day and a night (or even less, a few hours), while the longest conceivable would be the life span of a human being; and between the two are countless degrees. Whoever anticipates no more than a month is closer to realizing his goal than one who looks forward to a year. Whoever limits himself to forty days on account of the promise to Moses—may peace be upon him—is far off the mark, for that event by itself does not offer any clarification of the extent to which one may entertain expectations. It is rather that Moses deserved to attain [294] what was promised, though he did not achieve it until after forty days, in accordance with a secret accord with him including related features of the *sunna* of God Most High in ordering affairs.[63] As the Prophet—may peace be upon him—said: "God kneaded the clay of Adam with his hand for forty days,"[64] but only because that clay had to be kneaded since it had been stored in a place for some time before it reached the point mentioned.

In effect, only those with diminished judgment of heart and who rely on means store up for more than a year, and they are quite outside the station of trust in God, bereft as they are of any certainty in comprehending the ordering proper to authentic trust in hidden means. For the means [available] to one belonging to the elevated [states] and to almsgivers are normally repeated year by year. So whoever stores up for less than a year belongs to the grade of those whose expectations are short, while one whose expectations are for two months is not at the level of one whose expectations are for one month, or of one whose expectations are for three—but between the two. Nothing keeps one from storing up except that his expectations are foreshortened, though it is best when one does not store up at all. Yet the weaker his heart the less he stores up, even if it were better for him to save more. The story is told of a poor man whose corpse the Prophet ﷺ commissioned ʿAlī—may God bless his face—and Usāma to wash. They washed it and wrapped it in the Prophet's ﷺ mantle, and when he buried it he said to his companions: "When he rises on the day of resurrection his face will be like the moon on a night of full moon, and if he had nothing properly his own, his face at the resurrection will be like the morning sun." And we said: "How so, O Messenger of God?" He answered: "He was a faster and a keeper of many night vigils, and constantly remembered God Most High, yet when winter came he stored his summer cloak until next summer and when summer came he stored his winter cloak until next winter." Then he added: "But at least you can profit from his certainty and the excellence of his patience."[65]

Water cans and knives and other things needed to survive are hardly at issue here; holding onto them does not diminish one's degree [of trust in God]. Of course, one does not need a winter cloak in the summer, but this has to do with those whose hearts will not be disturbed by foregoing storing things, and who do not raise their souls to the hands of men, since their hearts are inclined to authentic trust in God. If they should sense their souls becoming agitated in such a way as to remove their hearts from prayer, recollection, and meditation, then it is better for them to store things up. And if one has acquired a place in the country, let him take full possession of it according to his needs, and if his heart is fully occupied with it, that will be better for him. For the goal is that the heart be freed to devote itself exclusively to recollection of God, yet some individuals occupy themselves with maintaining possessions while others are taken up with having nothing.

What one must beware of is what diverts one from God—Great and Glorious; it is not the world itself that one must beware of—neither its presence nor its absence. So the Messenger of God—may the blessing and peace of God Most High be on him and his family—was sent to all sorts of men—merchants, professionals, people of various occupations, and manual laborers—and he never demanded that merchants give up trading nor professionals their professions, nor did he require those not so engaged to engage themselves in these works. Rather he called everyone to God Most High, guiding them to success and to salvation by turning their hearts away from this world to God Most High, for the ground of devotion to God—Great and Glorious—is the heart, so the right thing for the weak [of heart] is to store up what they need, just as the right thing for the strong [of heart] is to forego storing up anything.

All of this sets a standard for single persons. Those responsible for a family do not depart from trust in God when they store up food for a year for their family, compelled as they are to do so by the weakness of their family members as well as needing to put their own hearts to rest. Storing up more than that nullifies trust in God, for the means recur year by year, and storing up beyond those means bespeaks a weakness of heart and runs contrary to the strength of trust in God. For one who trusts in divine providence is identical with one who believes in divine unity, with a strong heart and a soul at rest in the face of God Most High, and the fruits of his order beyond the presence of visible means. For the Messenger of God—may blessing and peace be on him and his family—stored up food for his family for a year, while he forbade Umm Ayman and others to save anything for the following day. He even forbade Bilāl to save a piece of bread with which to break the fast, saying, "Give it away, Bilāl, and do not fear being left bereft by the One who sits on the throne."[66] He also said: "When someone asks you, do not refuse; and when someone gives to you [295] do not hoard it."[67]

One should emulate the master of those who trust in God [Muhammad], whose expectations were so short that when he urinated he would purify himself with sand, even though water was nearby, saying: "Who knows? I may not reach it?"[68] So Muhammad—may the blessing and peace of God be on him and his family—though he saved, did not thereby diminish his trust in God, since he did not put his confidence in what he had stored up, but renounced it to teach the strong in his community. For the strong ones in his community are weak in comparison with his strength, so did he store up for his family for a year because of the weakness of his heart or that of his family? That it was not on account of the weakness of his family one knows from a hadith: "God Most High loves that you give him permission, just as he loves when you give him determination."[69] He perfumes the hearts of the weak so that they do not end up in desperation and hopelessness, thus foregoing the good, which they can easily do in the face of their inability to achieve [higher] levels. None but the Messenger of God ﷺ was sent to bring compassion to all the inhabitants of the world, of different races and levels. If you understand this you will know that saving is harmful to some people and not to others.

In proof of that, there is the story which Abū Umāma al-Bāhilī recounted. One of the people who lived on the porch of the mosque [in Medina] died and no winding sheet was found for him. The Prophet ﷺ said: "Look though his clothing." When they found two dinars inside his tunic, he said: "[The equivalent of] two brands!"[70] Yet other Muslims died and left possessions behind and he did not say that of them. That suggests two ways of understanding [what he said], for the person's condition could imply one of two states: [1] that [the Prophet ﷺ] meant two brands from hellfire, recalling what the Most High said: "Their foreheads and their flanks and their backs will be branded therewith" [9:35]. That would be the case if his state appeared to be one of renunciation, meditation, and trust in God, though he lacked them all; it would indicate a kind of deceit. Or [2] if there were no question of deceit, what is meant is a lessening of the level of perfection, as two brands on one's face would in effect lessen its beauty, and that would not be a matter of deceit. Each thing which a man leaves behind him means a diminishment in his rank in the next world, since nothing is given to one in this world without proportionally diminishing him in the next.

Regarding the explanation of a manner of saving which leaves the heart unencumbered with storing things up, and so need not nullify trust in God, there is the story told by Bishr [b. al-Ḥarīth al-Ḥāfī]. Al-Ḥusayn al-Maghāzilī, one of the companions, said: "I was with him one morning when a middle-aged man came into him, tawny of complexion and with a sparse beard, and Bishr came up to him, saying: 'I saw him standing there before anyone else'." Al-Ḥusayn continued: "He gave me a handful of dirhams and said to me: 'Buy us some of the best delicacies you can'. No one had ever said anything like that to me. So I bought some food and put it in front of him and ate it with him. I did not see him eating with anyone else. We ate what we needed and much food was left over. The man took it and gathered it into his cloak and took it with him as he left. I wondered at that and felt some distaste for him because of it. Bishr said to me: 'Do you perchance disapprove of what he did'? I answered: 'Indeed. He took the rest of the food without permission'. Bishr said: 'That is our brother Fath al-Mawṣilī. He came to visit us today from Mawṣil for he wanted to teach us that trust in God can be helped rather than harmed by storing things up'."[71]

[3.3] *On making use of means to repel injury and resist danger*

Know that injury may spell danger to life or property, and it does not belong to the conditions of trust in God to renounce, on principle, all means of repelling it. Regarding danger to life, it is like one who sleeps in the midst of wild animals or in the dry bed of a stream or under an overhanging wall or a broken roof. All that is prohibited, and one who does it has already [296] exposed his life to destruction to no purpose. In fact, these means can be divided into effective ones, probable ones, and illusory ones. One of the conditions of trust in God is to renounce illusory means; that is, all those related to repelling injury by means of branding or incantations. Some invoke branding or spells beforehand to repel the danger they anticipate, while others employ them after the danger emerges to eliminate it. The Messenger of God always describes those who trust in God as renouncing branding, incantations, and the omens of birds. He does not describe them as people who go out into a cold place without wearing a cloak, for wearing a cloak repels the anticipated cold. One will be able to understand all means in a similar way. So encouraging one to eat garlic, for example, when he goes out on a journey in winter, so as to stimulate the power of heat within him, could perhaps be tantamount to becoming absorbed in means and relying on them, and so verge on proximity to branding, by contrast with the cloak.

Now renouncing means of repelling [injury] has a clear sense when the injury comes to one from a human being: indeed, when it is possible for one to endure patiently or to repel and take revenge, a condition of trust in God is to suffer and to endure patiently, as God Most High says: *Choose Him alone for your defender, and bear with patience what they utter* [73:9-10]. And again: *We will endure patiently whatever harm you do to us. Let it be in God that trust is placed by those who will to trust* [14:12]; and: *Disregard their truculence and put your trust in God* [33:48]; and: *Have patience* [*O Muhammad*], *even as the stout of heart among the messengers* [*had patience*] [46:35]; and finally: *How blessed the reward of those who toil, who persevere and put their trust in their Lord* [29:28-29].

These things concern injury at the hands of people; as for patiently enduring injury from animals, wild beasts or scorpions, renouncing repelling them does not belong to trust in God at all, nor it is of any utility whatsoever. Not to intend to make any effort or not to renounce making an effort come to the same thing, though one or the other may be more supportive of religion; indeed the way of ordering means here is like the way one orders them in working for a livelihood and acquiring what one needs, so let us not prolong things by repeating them. Similarly for means employed to protect one's property: it does not diminish trust in God to secure the door to one's home when one goes out, or to hobble a camel, for these means are known to be part of the *sunna* of God Most High, whether they be effective or probably means. The Prophet ﷺ addressed this when a Bedouin had left a camel untended, saying: "I place my trust in God," by responding: "Hobble it and then trust in God."[72] And the Most High says: *Take your precautions* [4:71]; and regarding the manner of executing the "prayer of fear"[73] He also says: *Take up your arms* [4:102]; and again: *Make ready against them armed force and mounted cavalry to your utmost ability* [8:60]. And the Most High said to Moses—peace be upon him: *Set forth with my servants by night* [44:23]. Protection of the night consists in hiding oneself from the eyes of enemies and also [removing oneself from] certain means, as the Messenger of God hid in a cave, concealed from the eyes of enemies and so repelling harm.[74] Taking up arms during prayer is not an effective repellent like killing an animal or a scorpion, for that effectively repels [the harm]; while taking up arms represents only a probable means. We have already explained how probable means are like effective ones; it is the illusory ones which one must renounce, as contrary to trust in divine providence.

Now you might say: It has been said of certain ones that a lion put his paws on their shoulders without their being agitated. I would respond: It is said about certain ones that they ride lions and make them subservient; but there is no need to deceive yourselves about that station.[75] For even if it were [297] authentic in itself, it would hardly be healthy to imitate a path which one learns about from someone else. That station is marked by an abundance of miracles and is certainly not a condition for trusting in God; it is rather replete with secrets which cannot be divined by those who have not attained it. You might also say: What are the signs by which I could know that I had attained it? I would respond: One who attains it does not need to look for signs. However, one of the signs of that station does in fact precede it: that a dog become subject to you, a dog which is always with you, indeed inside your skin—named Anger [or Resentment]. [Normally] it does not stop biting you and biting others. But if this dog becomes subservient to you to the extent that when it becomes agitated and irritated, it will be subject to you instantaneously, then you may enhance your rank to the point where a lion, the very king of beasts, will be subject to you. It is more appropriate that the dog in your house be subject to you than a dog in the desert; but it is even more appropriate that the dog inside your skin be subject to you than the dog in your house. For if the dog within is not subject to you, how can you hope to make the dog outside subject to you?

Now you may say: if one who trusts in God takes up weapons as protection against enemies, secures his door as a protection against theft, and hobbles his camel to keep it from running away, what can trusting in God mean? I would respond: Such a one is trusting in God by knowledge and by state. With regard to *knowledge*, it is knowing that if the thief is repelled, securing the door did not suffice to repel him, but that he is only repelled by God Most High himself repelling him. For how many doors have been secured to no avail? How many camels have been hobbled and yet have died or escaped? Or how many have taken up arms only to be killed or overcome? So do not be consumed with these means, but with the cause which makes the means to be means, as we presented in the story of the lawyer and the legal action: when those who were present brought forward the charges, [the accused] did not put his trust in himself or in his documents, but in the sufficiency of the lawyer and his skills. With regard to *state*, one is content with whatever God Most High decides for him as well as for his household, and says: O God, if you exercise Your authority over what is in the house, then let whomever takes anything be on the way to You, and I shall be content with your judgment. For I do not know whether what you give me is a gift such that You will not take it back, or a loan and a trust which You will reclaim. Nor do I know whether I shall be given sustenance or whether You will have anticipated from eternity sustenance for someone else; but however You have decided, I shall be content with it. I did not secure the door as a protection from Your decision or [to show] resentment of it, but rather as a way of being attuned to the decision of Your *sunna* in arranging the means [as You do], and so trusting only in You, the cause of all means.

When this is his state, and his knowledge is aligned as we have already noted, he does not breach the limits of trust in God by hobbling a camel, taking up arms, or securing doors. So if he returns and finds his furnishings in his house, he should consider that a fresh grace on the part of God Most High. And if he does not find them, but rather finds that they have been stolen, then let him look to his heart. If he finds it content and even happy with that, knowing that God does not take from him without adding to his sustenance in the next world, then his station of trust in God is genuine and its sincerity is manifested to him. But if his heart is saddened at the sight, and he finds it difficult to be patient, then it will be clear to him that he is not sincere in the claim to trust in God. For trust in divine providence is a station following that of renunciation [*zuhd*], and renunciation is only genuine when one is not saddened by what one loses in this world nor made happy by what one is given, but indeed quite the opposite. So how can one [who has not reached this station] genuinely trust in God? He may have attained the station of patience if he conceals his reaction and is not heard complaining, or if he does not expend a great deal of effort in searching for and ferreting out [the culprit]. But if he cannot manage that, and his heart feels offended so that he begins to complain with his tongue, and engages in a thorough investigation with all the means at his disposal, then the robbery will have maximized the sin in him to the point that he is seen to be incapable of any of the stations, and has been deceiving himself in all that he pretended to be. After this, he will have to dedicate himself not to believe in his pretensions, and not to fall into the snare of their deceptions. For they amount to a betrayal: "inciting to evil" [12:53] yet claiming to be good.

You might ask: how could one who trusts in God have possessions so that they could be taken? I would answer that those who trust in God do not lack certain furnishings in their house, like a large bowl to eat out of and a jug to drink from, as well as a container for ritual purification and a traveling bag in which to keep provisions, and a walking stick with which to repel what may harm them—and other house furnishings of that sort necessary to subsist. It may be that possessions come into his hand, and he takes hold of them so that if he comes across someone in need he may pass them on to him, so one can hardly consider that saving something for this purpose nullifies one's trust in God. Nor is it a condition of trust in God to get rid of a jug [298] to drink from or a traveling bag for one's provisions. That rather concerns foodstuffs and any possession in excess of what may be considered necessary. For the *sunna* of God shows by experience that good things come to the poor who trust in God in the corner of the mosque, and the [same] *sunna* does not entail distributing one's jugs and other furnishings every day or even every week. And it is hardly a condition of trust in God that one be outside the *sunna* of God—Great and Glorious. So it was that when he traveled, al-Khawwas took with him rope, a cup, scissors and a needle, but no provisions, for the *sunna* of God Most High knows how to distinguish among such things.

You might ask: how is it conceivable that one not be sad and upset when someone takes the furnishings that one needs? If he had not wanted them, why had he held onto them and secured them by locking the door? And if he held onto them because he wanted them to fulfill his needs, how can his heart not be hurt or he not be sad about what has intervened between him and what he wants? I would respond: It could be that he kept them to help him in his religion, if he had come to think that it was good for him that those furnishings belonged to him, and that if it were not good for him then God Most High would not have given him sustenance or given him these things. He could substantiate that by the way in which God—Great and Glorious—had facilitated things for him. Furthermore, he had had delightful thoughts of God Most High as he thought that these things were a help to him and so [could be counted] among the means of religion. Yet such thoughts could hardly be decisive for him, since it could also be good for him to be tested by losing [these things], so that he would have to exert himself to attain his goal, and a great deal of effort and strain would be meritorious for him. For when God Most High used the power of the thief to take from him, his thinking was transformed, because he had trusted in God in all circumstances and always thought well of Him. So he said: if God—Great and Glorious—had not known that it was good for me to have had them up until now yet better for me not to have them now, He would not have taken them from me. One can conceive someone driving sadness away by thoughts like these, for in this way his happiness will be seen to have nothing to do with means as means, but only in so far as the cause of means had made them accessible by his providence or favor.

This is like the sick person in the hands of a sympathetic doctor, content with what he does for him. Should he prepare nourishment for him, he is happy, saying: "Had he not known that the nourishment would help me and that I would be able to take it, he would not have set it before me." And when he kept food away from him after that, he would be happy and say: "Were it not that the food would harm me and lead to my death, he would not have kept me from it." Unless one has faith in the graciousness of God Most High like the sick person has faith in the compassionate father versed in the knowledge of medicine, trust in God will never be genuine in him. Yet whoever knows God Most High, who knows His works and knows how His *sunna* works to the good of His servants, will never be made happy by means, for he cannot discern which means would be better for him. As ʿUmar—may God be pleased with him—said: "It is indifferent to me whether I become rich or poor, for I cannot discern which of them would be better for me."[76] Similarly, one who trusts in divine providence ought to be indifferent whether his goods are stolen or not, for he cannot discern which would be better for him in this world or the next. For how many goods in this world are a source of destruction for human beings! How many rich people are tempted to misfortune by their wealth and say: would that I were poor!

[3.31] *Explanation of the conduct of those who trust in divine providence when their goods are stolen*

[There are different] modes of conduct of one who trusts in God with regard to the furnishings of his house when he leaves it. First, that one secure the house without scrutinizing all the means of security, such as securing it from one's neighbors even while it is locked, or amassing many keys. Mālik b. Dīnār never locked his door but made it fast with a cord, saying: "But for the dogs, I would not even make it fast."[77] Second, that one not leave goods in the house to incite robbers to it, for it would constitute an occasion of sin for them, and refraining from it would be an occasion for arousing their desires. So it was that when the rightly guided al-Mughīra tried to give Mālik b. Dīnār a coffee pot, he said: "Keep it; I do not need it." Al-Mughīra said: "Why not?" He responded: "The enemy [Satan] has sown doubts in me that it might be stolen, so I want to be sure not to provoke the thief." Something allowed his heart to be taken up with scruples of Satan regarding its being stolen, and to that Abū Sulaymān said: "That stems from the weakness of Sufi hearts, itself a result of renouncing the world. What is it to him if someone steals it?"[78]

Third, when one is obliged to leave something in the house, he must resolve when he leaves it to be content with God's decision whether a thief will have access to it, and say: "What the thief takes either belongs to him by right or by the leave of God Most High, and if he is poor it can be alms for him." And it is even better if poverty is not made a condition; in fact, there are two ways of thinking about [the theft], depending on whether the one who takes it be wealthy or poor. [299] First, that possessing his goods will keep the man from further sin. It could be that he would no longer need to steal, that he would lose any further will to steal, and could even abandon his sinful ways of taking what is prohibited, once it was freely entrusted to him. Or second, that he would not harm another Muslim, in the sense that one's goods would be ransom for the goods of another Muslim. To the extent that one sees oneself protecting the goods of someone else by one's own goods, or sees [in the theft] a way of repelling the thief's sinful ways or of hiding them from him, one may well counsel Muslims to imitate the Prophet ﷺ when he says: "Help your brother, whether he be one who perpetrates or who suffers evil."[79] To help the evildoer is to prevent him from doing evil; and by refraining from it, one removes the evil and prevents it as well. Moreover, one may also be assured that this way of proceeding would in no way harm him, since no force is brought to bear on the thief and eternal judgment is in no way altered. Furthermore, one can be assured of renunciation by acting in this way, for when his property was taken he had seven hundred dirhams backing each dirham, for that had been his design and intent; and if he had not been robbed, he would have received his due in any case. Something similar is told in one of the traditions of the Prophet of God—may God's peace be upon him: whoever ejaculates and places semen where it properly belongs will be rewarded by a child being born to him from that intercourse, one who lives and dies in the way of God Most High; or it may be that none is born, since he had no concern for the child but only for the sexual intercourse. Creation, life, sustenance and enduring relationship were nothing to him, yet were [the child] to be created, it would be a reward for his action so that the action would not be nugatory.[80] So it is with the thief.

Fourth, should one find one's property stolen, he need not be sad but rather happy, if that be possible, and say: if there were no good in it, God Most High would not have taken it away.[81] Moreover, if he had not placed it in the service of God Most High, then he ought not go to great lengths in his search for it nor imagine the worst of [his fellow] Muslims. And if he had placed it in the service of God Most High, he should withdraw his petition, since he has already made it over as provision for his soul in the next life. Should it be returned to him, it would be more appropriate not to accept it after he had placed it in the service of God—Great and Glorious. But should he accept it, it belongs to him according to the literal understanding [of the law], because the right of possession perdures despite all that has taken place. But those who trust in God would hardly prefer this way of acting.

It is told of [ᶜAbdullah] b. ᶜUmar that his she-camel was stolen and he searched for it to the point of exhaustion. At that point he said: "Let it be for the cause of God Most High," and entered a mosque to pray two rakas when a man came to him and said: "O Abu ᶜAbd ar-Rahman, your she-camel is in a certain place." He put on his sandals, stood up, and then said: "I ask God's forgiveness!" and sat down. When he was asked: "Why don't you go get it?" he responded: "But I already said: 'Let it be for the cause of God'."[82] A sheikh said: "I saw one of my brothers in a dream after he had died, and said to him: 'What has God done with you?' He answered me: 'He has forgiven me and brought me into paradise and showed me my station there, and I have seen it'. Yet despite that he was melancholic and sad, so I said: 'But you said that He had forgiven you and that you had entered paradise, yet you are sad!' He sighed deeply and said: 'Indeed; and I shall not cease to be sad until the day of resurrection'; to which I said: 'Why is that?' He answered: 'As I was looking at my station in paradise, dwellings appeared to me in the uppermost heaven the likes of which I had never seen, and I was elated over them. Yet when I set myself to enter them, an announcement proclaimed from above: 'Keep him away from them, for these are not for him, since they are for those who have completed the journey'. When I asked: 'What is it to complete the journey?', it was said to me: 'You pledged something, saying 'it is for the cause of God' and then you took it back. If you had completed the journey, we would have brought you to completion'."[83]

It is related of one of God's servants in Mecca that he was sleeping next to a man who had his purse with him. The man awakened and missed his purse, and accused him of [taking] it, so he said to him: "How much was in your purse?" He told him, so he took him home and compensated him accordingly. Afterwards his companions informed him that it was they who had taken his purse, to play a joke on him. So he came with his companions to return the gold.

But the other refused it, saying: "Take it as a blessing! For it could not be that I would take back something given over to the cause of God—Great and Glorious." So he would not take it, and when they pressed him, he called his son and began to tie some purses together and delegated him to distribute them to the poor until nothing was left.[84] [300] Such was the character of those who preceded us. Similarly, whoever would take a loaf of bread to give it to a beggar, only to withdraw it from him out of disgust and take it home to give it to another beggar after he had already given it over, would do the same with dirhams, dinars, and other alms.

The fifth is the lowest level in that one does not curse the thief who wrongs him by taking [what is his]. If he did, that would nullify his trust in God and prove how unresigned and sad he was over what had been lost, as well as cancel any remuneration. And should [his reaction] be exaggerated he would also forfeit any reward he might have achieved by it. So in a report: "Whoever curses the one who does him harm has already taken his revenge."[85] It is told of Rabī'a b. Khuthaym that his horse, along with 20,000 [dirhams], was stolen while he was standing in place in public prayer. He did not cut short his prayer, nor did he bestir himself to look for it. When people came to him to console him, he said: "I have already seen what happened and that he set him free." One asked: "What keeps you from rebuking him?" To which he answered: "I was engaged in something which is dearer to me than that; I mean public prayer." So they began to curse him, but he said: "Don't do that! Rather say good things, for I have already given it over to him as alms."[86]

One of the [Sufi sheikhs] was asked, regarding something which had been stolen from him: "would you not curse the one who so harmed you?" And he replied: "It is hardly preferable that I be the one who helps Satan in this regard." Then they asked: "What would you do were he to return it to you?" He said: "I would neither take it nor renounce it, since I have already made it over to him." They said to another: "Let God Most High curse the one who harmed you!" But he said: "No one has harmed me. He has rather harmed himself. And as though it were not enough for the poor fellow to harm himself; he must even increase his share of evil!"[87] Some of them frequently berated al-Ḥujjāj regarding one of his brothers-in-law for his misdeed, to which he responded: "Don't trouble yourselves with berating him, for God Most High will take vengeance for al-Ḥujjāj on whomever violates what pertains to him, as He will do justice concerning whomever takes his money or his life-blood."[88] And in a report: "If someone continues to berate the one who harmed him for the harm he did, and curse him to the same extent that he originally harmed him, then the result is that the one who now does him harm is answerable for supplying him with the opportunity to retaliate against the one originally harmed."[89]

Sixth, one may be distressed for the thief on account of his disobedience and his opposition to the chastisement of God Most High, and thank God Most High when He makes him the one harmed rather than the one doing harm, so making him diminish in his life in this world but not diminish in his religion. When one of the people began to complain to a learned one that someone had waylaid him and taken his money, the one addressed said: "If your distress that someone felt it permissible to do this among Muslims is not greater than your anxiety over your money, then you are not well-disposed towards Muslims."[90] Some dinars were stolen from ᶜAlī b. al-Fudayl [b. ᶜIyād] as he was wandering about the [holy] house [in Mecca]. His father saw him and [noticed that] he was sad and in mourning. So he said: "ᶜAlī, are you mourning for the dinars?" He answered: "No, by God, but for the poor man who will be questioned on the day of resurrection and will have no excuse."[91] Another one of them was told: "Curse the one who harmed you!" He responded: "I am taken up with sadness for him rather than curses against him."[92] Now that was the manner of life displayed by our ancestors, and God was well pleased [*riḍā'*] with of all of them.

[3.4] *On the effort to remove harm, as in treatment of disease and similar things*

You should know that the means for making disease disappear can also be divided into [1] decisive means, like water for removing the harm of thirst, or bread for removing the harm of hunger; [2] likely means: regimes, cupping, drinking purgative medicines, and other medical means like treatment of chills by heat or fevers by cold, and all such means presumed in medicine; and [3] illusory means like cauterizing and incantations. With regard to decisive means, trust in God does not dispense with them; moreover, it is prohibited to dispense with them in danger of death. [301] With regard to illusory means, a condition of trusting in God is to dispense with them, as the Messenger of God ﷺ has described for those who would trust in God: the strongest prohibition is against cauterizing, next come incantations, with the omens of birds the lowest level.[93] Whoever believes in or trusts in these has reached the very bottom with regard to means.

So far as the middle level is concerned, these are likely [means], as in treatments presumed among doctors which utilize means, so having recourse to them is not inconsistent with trusting in God—by contrast with illusory ones. Nor is dispensing with them prohibited, by contrast with decisive means; but there are certain advantages to utilizing them in particular situations and for particular persons, so this level is between the other two. The actions of the Messenger of God—may God's praise be upon him and his family, as well as what he said and commanded, all go to prove that treatment is not inconsistent with trusting in God. As for his statements, he said: "Except for death, there is no malady without a treatment—those who know one know it; those who do not know one are ignorant of it."[94] He also said—peace be upon him: "Make use of treatments, for God created maladies and treatments."[95] Someone asked him about treatments and incantations: whether they contradicted in any way the decree of God? He answered: "They lie within the decree of God."[96] And in a well-known report: "I passed through hosts of angels [on my night journey] only to have them all say: 'Order your community to use cupping'."[97] In the hadith he ordered this: "Let them cup on the seventeenth, nineteenth, and twenty-first [day of the month], for you will not have so much blood taken out of you as to kill you."[98] He also mentioned that the removal of blood is the cause of death and that it kills by the will of God Most High, yet made clear that blood-letting spelled deliverance from death. There is no distinction made among taking deadly blood from [beneath] the skin, removing a scorpion from under one's clothing, or removing a serpent from the house—and it is hardly a condition of trusting in God to forego such actions. It is similar to pouring water on a fire to quench it and so minimize its harm in the house to the point of stopping it. It can hardly belong to trusting in God to dispense with the *sunna* of the One in whom we trust! In a decisive report it says: "Whoever engages in cupping on the third day [Tuesday], the seventeenth of the month, has a cure for illness for a year."[99]

Concerning the Prophet's commands—peace be upon him—he ordered several of his companions to take treatment and to follow a diet.[100] He also cut the vein of Sa'īd b. Mu'ādh to bleed him; and he cauterized Sa'īd b. Zurāra.[101] And he said to ʿAlī—may God be pleased with him—who had inflammation of the eye: "Don't eat on account of that!"—meaning fresh dates. And "Everything of that sort is not for you," meaning chard cooked with barley meal.[102] When he saw Ṣuhayb [b. Sīnān], who had an eye ailment, eating dried dates he said to him: "You are eating dried dates [302] yet your eye is inflamed." "But I eat on the other side," he answered, and the Prophet ﷺ smiled.[103]

Concerning his actions—may God's blessing and peace be upon him, it is reported in a hadith transmitted by the family of the Prophet ﷺ that he blackened his eyelids each morning, was bled each month, and drank a remedy each year. He also underwent treatment several times for scorpions and suchlike.[104] It is told of him that he was afflicted with headaches whenever inspiration came down upon him, so he covered it over with henna.[105] And in a report it says that when they removed a boil from him they put henna on it, and then put humus on the boil they had removed from him.[106] A great deal, quite beyond enumerating, has been related about his treatments and his commands concerning such things; indeed a book has been published on it, entitled "The Medicine of the Prophet."[107]

A learned man related from the stories of the Jews [*Isrā'īliāt*] that Moses—peace be upon him—fell ill with a disease, and when some Jews found out about his illness they came to him and said: "If you will let yourself be treated in a certain way, you will be cured." To which he replied: "I will not undertake treatment; let Him cure me without any treatment." Ye his illness lingered, so they said to him: "The treatment for this illness is well-known and proven; we have undergone it and been cured." But he said: "I will not [let myself] be treated." Yet the illness persisted, and God Most High revealed to him: "By My glory and greatness, I shall not cure you unless you undergo the treatment which they mentioned to you." So he said to them: "Treat me in the way you described." They treated him and he recovered. He became troubled in himself over this, and God Most High revealed to him: "Do you want to nullify My wisdom by your trusting in Me? Who is it who has supplied drugs useful to all sorts of things?"[108]

It is said in a hadith that one of the Prophets—peace be upon them—complained of an illness he had, and God Most High revealed to him: "Eat an egg." Another complained of weakness, and God Most High revealed to him: "Eat flesh with milk, for there is power in both of them." It is said that the weakness was impotence.[109] It is also said that some people complained to their prophet that their children were ugly, so God Most High revealed to him: "Make them give their pregnant wives quince to eat, for it makes children fair." They did that for three or four months while God Most High was forming the offspring. So they resolved that pregnant wives should eat quince, and those confined to childbirth fresh dates.

In this way it is made clear that the One who makes causes to be causes carries out His *sunna* by linking whatever is caused to their causes as a demonstration of divine wisdom. So it is that treatments are causes subservient to the authority of God Most High, like all other means.[110] Just as bread is a treatment for hunger and water for thirst, so oxymel is a treatment for jaundice and scammony for diarrhea—yet with two qualifications. First, the remedy for hunger and thirst by bread and water is clear and manifest and perceived by everyone, while the remedy for jaundice by oxymel is known only to a few specialists, yet whoever becomes aware of the second kind [of connection] by experience links it, so far as he is concerned, with the first. [303] Secondly, the fact that treatments purge—that oxymel can suppress jaundice—is a function of other conditions in the body and causes in conjunction, and it is often difficult to be apprised of all such conditions. It may be that one or another missing condition will keep the treatment from purging. With regard to quenching thirst, however, that does not require many conditions other than water, though there could be certain obstacles whose presence assured the malady of thirst no matter how much water one drank—but that is rare. In any case, the failure of causes can be restricted to these two factors. What is caused follows the cause without exception once the conditions of the cause have been fulfilled, and all that is according to the ordering of the One who makes causes to be causes, subservient to Him. His arrangement is according to the judgment of his wisdom and the perfection of his decree.[111] So there is no harm for those trusting in God to make use of them, provided they fix their gaze on the One who makes causes to be causes, rather than on the doctor or the treatment.

It is told of Moses—may God's blessing and peace be upon him—that when he said: "O Lord, whence come illness and treatment?" the Most High answered: "From Me." "What then is the work of physicians?" Moses asked, and [God] said: "They consume their sustenance, offering treatment to the souls of my servants until My healing or My judgment is forthcoming."[112] So the sense of trusting in God with regard to remedies is the trust of knowledge and of a state, as we treated earlier in the chapters concerning actions to ward off harm or to secure one's advantage. So it is not a condition of such trust that one completely renounce treatments.

Now you may say: cauterizing is certainly an evident and useful means. I would respond: not at all! For among the evident means one finds bleeding, cupping, drinking remedies, and hot and cold drinks. With regard to cauterizing, if something like it were an evident means, why is it not employed in more countries? It is seldom utilized in many countries, though it is the custom among Turks and the Bedouin. It is one of the illusory means, like incantations, except that it can be distinguished from them by the fact that it consists in burning a person on the spot, even though he has no need of it. For there is no pain treated by cauterizing which cannot be treated otherwise, in a way which does not involve burning. Moreover, burning by fire causes a wound destructive of one's physical constitution, so one should be aware of promoting its use, especially given that it is useless! By contrast, it is unlikely that bloodletting or cupping will become extensive, and nothing other than these two can substitute for them. For that reason, the Messenger of God—may God's blessing and peace be upon him—has prohibited cauterizing but not incantations.[113] Yet both of them are inconsistent with trusting in God.

It is related that ʿImrān b. Ḥaṣīn was sick and they urged him to be cauterized, but he refused. But they did not let up, and pressed the duty upon him, until he was cauterized. Then he said: "It used to be that I saw light and heard sounds, and angels comforted me. Since I was cauterized, I have been cut off from all that." He also said: "I underwent cauterization but—by God—without luck or success." Then he turned away from that and turned to God Most High, and God Most High responded to him by placing him among the ranks of angels. He said to Muṭarrif b. ʿAbdullāh: "Do you not see the angelic [gifts] with which God has honored me in that God Most High has returned them to me?"—after he had reported their loss to Him.[114] In sum, cauterizing and such remedies do not benefit those who trust in God, for we must contrive to place them in the [divine] arrangement [of things]. As a result, it is blameworthy, and that proves the evil of depending on means and putting one's trust in them—as God alone knows!

[3.41] *Explaining that dispensing with treatment belongs to some states and demonstrates the power of God, and how that does not contradict the practice of the Messenger of God ﷺ*

You should know that countless of our ancestors made use of treatments, yet a great many of the leading [sheikhs] also renounced them. But you may esteem that to be a shortcoming, since if it were a perfection the Messenger of God—peace be upon him—would have renounced treatment, for there cannot be a state of trusting in God greater than his. It is told of Abu Bakr—may God be pleased with him—that he was asked: "Should we call a doctor for you?" and he answered: "The doctor already saw me and said: 'I am doing what I intend.'"[115] When someone asked Abu'l-Dardā' in the course of his illness: "What do you complain about?" he answered: "My sins." So they asked: "What do you desire?" and he said: "The forgiveness of my Lord." When they asked him: "Should we not call a doctor for you?" he replied: "A doctor made me ill."[116] When both of his eyes were inflamed, Abū Dharr was asked: "Are you treating them?" to which he answered: "I am distracted from them." So they asked: "Have you asked God Most High to cure you?" and he said: "I have asked Him for things more important to me than [my eyes]."[117] [304] Rabī'a b. Khuthaym was overtaken with lameness, and was asked whether he would submit to treatments. He responded: "I was intent on it, but then I recalled [the tribes of] ʿA'ād and Thamūd, and the dwellers of ar-Rass, and many generations in between'[25:38]: how there were doctors among them yet both healers and healed were destroyed, and that the omens of birds profited them nothing."[118] Aḥmad b. Ḥanbal used to say: "I prefer that those committed to trusting in God and journeying on this path renounce treatments rather than drink remedies and things of that sort."[119] When he was ill, he would say nothing at all to the doctor about it if he asked him. Sahl [at-Tustarī] was asked: "When is a servant's trust in God authentic?" He answered: "When illness befalls him and his property is diminished, yet he is not inclined to be preoccupied with his condition but rather attends to the way in which God Most High sustains him."[120]

So some among our ancestors renounced remedies when they considered them, and others even despised them. Yet we can set forth a perspective which embraces both the practice of the Messenger of God—may God's blessing and peace be upon him—and their practices by enumerating the ways of dispensing with treatment, giving [six] reasons for doing so. First, if the sick person is visited with an unveiling in which the end of his life is revealed to him, so that treatment would be of no use to him. That can be made known to him sometimes in a reliable communication, sometimes by way of conjecture and surmising, and sometimes by an authentic unveiling. It is likely that the righteous one [Abū-Bakr]—may God be pleased with him—

renounced treatment for this reason. For he was one of those who received revelations; he said to ʿĀisha—may God be pleased with her—on the subject of inheritance: "They are both your sisters," when she had but one sister. But her mother was pregnant and she gave birth to a girl, and he knew that she was pregnant with a girl because it had been unveiled to him. Nor is it unlikely that the end of his life was not also revealed to him; otherwise it would be unthinkable that he reject treatment, given the witness of the Messenger of God—may God's blessing and peace be upon him—both ordering and undergoing treatment.

Second, that the sick person may be absorbed in his [spiritual] state and fearful of his sins and the knowledge God Most High has of them, so that he will be oblivious to the distress of illness: a heart so occupied with one's spiritual state can hardly devote itself to treatments. That is what the words of Abū Dharr express when he said: "I am distracted from [my inflamed eyes];" and the words of Abu'l-Dardā' when he said: I complain about my sins." His heart was in distress, fearful of his sins more than of the pain of his bodily illness. Such a one is like a strong man stricken by a death even stronger than he, or like a frightened person approaching the king of kings to be executed: when he is asked: "Won't you have something to eat? Are you hungry?" he will answer: "I am distracted from the pain of hunger." But it is hardly that he denies food being useful to counteract hunger; he is not contesting that one should eat! Close to this is the way Sahl [at-Tustarī] became enraged when he was asked: "What about some nourishment [*qaūt*]?" He responded: "That reminds me of *the Living and Self-existent One* [*al-Qayyūm*] [2:255]."[121] So they said: "We asked you about sustenance [*qawām*]" to which he responded: "Sustenance is knowledge." But they said: "We asked you about food [*qaūt*]," to which he answered: "Food is remembrance [of God's names: *dhikr*];" to which they retorted: "We asked you about feeding the body." He said in response: "What is the body to you? Whoever cares for it first of all will be caring for it at the end. When illness enters it, return it to the One who made it. Don't you see that when a product is deficient they return it to the one who made it so that it may be repaired?"

Third, the illness may be chronic, and the treatment indicated for it only of illusory usefulness relative to the illness, like cauterizing or the omens of birds, so that those who trust in God would renounce it. This is what Rabī'a b. Khuthaym alluded to when he said: "I recalled A'ād and Thamūd; there were doctors among them yet both healers and healed were destroyed"—that is, that treatment is not [totally] trustworthy. And this may be the case with regard to the treatment itself, or it may be that the sick person has but little practice in study and scant experience with illness. So it would not occur to him to think that the treatment could be useful. No doubt physicians have greater experience relying on treatments than others do, and confidence and knowledge are a function of reliance, while reliance is a function of experience. This is the reason why most of those who renounce treatment among servants and ascetics do so: they keep away from treatments as something illusory, with no basis for the claims made for them. That is a sound response to some treatments where one knows the origin of the medicine, yet not for all. Moreover, one who is not a physician tends to see everything in an [undifferentiated] glance, so that he sees [the practice of undergoing] treatments as absorbing one in means, like [having recourse to] cauterizing and the omens of birds, so he renounces it, trusting in God.

Fourth, it may be that the servant intends, by renouncing treatment, to prolong the illness in order to gain the merit of illness [endured] with admirable patience—seeing it as a trial [305] sent by God Most High to test his patience, or an opportunity to test his own capacity for patience. A great many references have been made to the merits of illness; let us begin with that of the Prophet—

may God's blessing and peace be upon him: "We, as companions of the Prophets, will be tested more than ordinary people, and one example after another tests the servant according to the measure of his faith: if his faith is solid the test will be difficult; if his faith is weak the trial will be mitigated."[122] And in a report: "God Most High tests His servants with trials, as each one of you tests his gold in fire: some of them come out like shining gold, others less so, and still others black and burned."[123] In a hadith transmitted by the family of the Prophet ﷺ it is said: "If God Most High loves a servant, He tests him: if he is patient He chooses him; if he is perfectly content [*riḍā'*], He selects him."[124] The Prophet—may God's blessing and peace be upon him—said: "Do you love to be like wandering asses, neither sick nor ailing?"[125]

Ibn Masa'ūd said—may God be pleased with him: "You will find believers to be healthier in their hearts as they are sicker in their bodies, while hypocrites will be healthier in body and sicker at heart."[126] To the extent that sickness and trials are highly praised, people prefer sickness and seize the opportunity to gain the merit of patience from it. And of those who are ill, some will conceal it, never mentioning it to a doctor, and suffer the illness perfectly content with the judgment of God Most High, understanding that the Truth [*al-Ḥaqq*] can prevail over his heart in such a way as to divert the illness from it, since it only affects his extremities.[127] They know that their participation in communal prayer is more beneficial, in the face of the judgment of God Most High, undertaken seated with patience than it would be standing whole and healed. Thus a most trustworthy hadith: "God Most High says to the angels: 'write down for my servant the good things he has done, for he is in bondage to Me. When I set him free I shall exchange superior flesh for his flesh, superior blood for his blood, and when I take him to Myself I will take him to My mercy'."[128] And the Prophet—may God's blessing and peace be upon him—said: "The most beneficial actions are those to which souls are coerced," by which he is said to mean whatever affects one by way of illness or injury. These are alluded to by the saying of the Most High: *It may well be that something you hate is nevertheless good for you* [2:216].[129]

Sahl [at-Tustarī] said: "If one is too weak to perform prescribed actions or incapable of fulfilling their religious duty, then renouncing treatment is better than undertaking treatment for the sake of performing prescribed actions." For he had a debilitating illness for which he did not undergo treatment, even though he treated people for it. When he saw a person praying seated, and unable to carry out the works of piety on account of his illnesses, yet who submitted to treatment so that he might stand at prayer and rouse himself to the prescribed actions, he wondered about that, saying: "Praying seated while perfectly content with one's condition is more beneficial than undergoing treatment to restore one's strength to pray standing." And to one who inquired about drinking remedies, he said: "Everything which enters into something as a remedy bestows a capacity from God Most High on those who are weak; it is more beneficial if there is nothing entering. For if one takes something as a remedy, even if it be cold water, he will be asked [at the judgment]: 'Why did you take it?' But if one takes nothing, nothing will be asked of him."[130] It was his teaching, and that of the school of Baṣri, that [wayward inclinations of the] soul were diminished by hunger and breaking one's desires, so they understood that the smallest of the works of the heart—such as patience, perfect contentment, and trusting in God—were more beneficial than heaps of works [306] undertaken by one's limbs. And illness does not prevent works of the heart, unless the pain of it be overwhelming.

Fifth, it may be that a person had accumulated guilt and was afraid on that account, and unable to expiate for it, so he would see in a prolonged illness a way of doing penance, and so would forego treatment lest the illness cease too quickly. As the Prophet—may God's blessing and peace be upon him—put it: "Let the fever and the state it engenders not cease for a person until he proceeds from the earth as one purified from his guilt and without offense."[131] And in a prophetic tradition: "Fever for one day is expiation for one year."[132] It is said [in explanation] that this is because it breaks down one's power for a year, or that a human being has 360 joints, and the fever enters all of them, bringing pain to each one of them, so that each single pain amounts to a day's penance.[133] When the Prophet—may God's blessing and peace be upon him—mentioned fever as expiation for sin, Zayd b. Thābit asked his Lord—Great and Glorious—that he might never cease to be feverish. So the fever never left him until he died—may God have mercy on him! Some of the itinerant Anṣāri asked that as well, and the fever never left them.[134] So when the Prophet—may God's blessing and peace be upon him—said: "Should God take away one's own eyes, there is no fitting reward short of paradise," it is said there were some Anṣāri who wanted to be blind. And Jesus—peace be upon him—said: "One who is not happy when misfortune or illness overtakes his body or his possessions, in such a way that he might anticipate thereby penance and atonement, can hardly be counted as learned."[135] It is related that Moses—peace be upon him—saw a person sorely tested and said: "O Lord, take pity on him," and the Most High said: How can I take pity on one on whom I have already taken pity—that is, in atoning for his sin and elevating his station?"[136]

Sixth, it may be that one is conscious within himself of the stirring of wantonness and tyranny over a long period of health, so that he would renounce treatment fearful lest the illness quickly cease and that carelessness, wantonness and tyranny become habitual with him; or that his optimism be extended in such a way as to put off his perception of the passage of time and the superiority of blessings. For health is like strength of attributes in inciting passion, moving desires, and motivating one to sin; or at the very least one is moved to take one's enjoyment in permissible things. But to do so is to miss favorable opportunities [lit, 'times'] and forego the immense profit from countering one's lower powers [*nafs*] and all that accompanies doing those things that are prescribed. So it is that God wishes the good of those who serve Him, yet not sparing them the counsel of illness and misfortune; and to that effect it is said: "Believers will not be without pain or illness or error."[137] And it has been related: "God Most High said: 'Poverty is my prison and illness my constraint; with these I withhold those whom I love from [attachment to] My creation'."[138]

Now if one is withheld by illness from tyranny and the domination of sin, what good is greater than that? Whoever is so fearful of his lower powers [*nafs*] as to guard against them by foregoing treatment hardly needs to occupy himself with remedies. One of those who know [*ᶜārafūn*] said to a man: "How have you been since I [last saw you]?" The other responded: "In good health." He said: "If you have not sinned against God Most High, then you are in good health; but if you have sinned against Him, what illness is worse than sin? No one can excuse sinning against God."[139] When ᶜAlī—may God honor him—saw the adornment of the Nabateans in Iraq on a feast day, he inquired: "What is this show they are putting on?" They said in reply: "O leader of the faithful, this is a day of festival for them." ᶜAlī responded: "Any day on which one does not sin against God is a feast day for us."[140] [307]

The Most High said: *You broke discipline just when God set before your very eyes the thing you longed to see* [3:152]; to which someone responded: "good health." *But No! man is perversely assertive, thinking himself his own lord* [96:6-7]—and that is how it is when good health leads one to assume [an air of] independence. One of them remarked: *Pharaoh said: 'I am your supreme lord'* [79:24] only on account of a prolonged period of good health. For four hundred years no one had challenged his sovereignty, nor did his body suffer fever or were his veins punctured, so he implored the divinity—God's curse be upon him!—that if he were to take away his daily migraine, that would distract him from the benefits of having to call on the divinity."[141] The Prophet—may God's blessing and peace be upon him—said: "Intensify your recollection on the One who cuts short pleasure."[142] It is said: "Fever is a scout for death,"[143] for it reminds one of it and resists procrastination. The Most High says: *Do they not see that they are being put to the test time and again? Yet they are still without repentance, nor do they call God to mind* [9:126]. It is said: "They are tested by the illnesses which they experience." It is also said: "Should a person beset with two illnesses not turn in repentance, an angel of death will say to him: 'O heedless one, I sent you messenger after messenger and you were not worthy of them."[144]

That is the reason why our ancestors were distressed when a year went by and they were not visited with some diminishment in their person or their property. They said: "The believer will not miss being startled by a surprise or visited by a trial every forty days."[145] So it is related that ᶜAmmār b. Yāsir married a woman who was not sick, so he divorced her. And of the Prophet ﷺ it is said that a woman was proposed to him and her attributes recounted in such a way as to incite him to marry her. But when it was said that she had no hint of illness, he said: "Then I have no need of her."[146] The Prophet ﷺ was speaking of sickness, when a man said: "What is a headache? I have never experienced one." The Blessed One of God ﷺ said to him: "Away from me! Whoever wishes to point out to a person something destined to the fire of hell, let him point out such a one!"[147] So it is related in a report: "Fever is the lot of every believer from the fire of hell."[148] In a hadith it is told of Anas and ᶜAisha—may God be pleased with them both—that someone asked: "O Messenger of God, will there be others along with the martyrs on the day of resurrection?" And he answered: "Indeed, those who recall death twenty times each day." Or in another expression: "Those who recall their sins and are saddened by them."[149] There is no doubt that those overcome with illness recall death, for illness brings many benefits: consider how many renounce strategies to foreshorten its duration when they see their souls strengthened by it? For it is not that they consider the remedies deficient; indeed, how could they when the Prophet—may God's blessing and peace be upon him—engaged in them?

[3.42] *Explanations countering those who say that foregoing treatment is more beneficial in every case*

Someone might say: the Messenger of God ﷺ engaged in them only to establish the *sunna* [of God] for those other than himself. For doing that represents a lower state; the stage for those who are stronger, as befits those who trust in God, is to renounce treatment. One could then say that it would follow as a condition of trusting in God to renounce cupping and puncturing veins to release blood. And were that a condition, then it would also be a condition that if a scorpion or [other] animal were to sting him, that he would not remove it from himself, for [308] how could one distinguish between [one taking] blood stinging one from within and a scorpion from outside? And were that also a condition of trusting in God, it would follow that one ought not alleviate the sting of thirst with water or the sting of hunger with bread or that of cold with heat—but no one would say that! [Assertions like these] do not discriminate among those stages, yet all of them are means established by the One who makes means to be means—the Most High and blessed One—and His *sunna* is carried out by means of them.

That these are not conditions of trust in God is proven by what is told of ʿUmar—may God be pleased with him—and the companions in the story of the plague. While they were proceeding to Syria and were nearing al-Jābiya, news reached them that many had died there in a devastating plague. The party divided in two, and one faction said: "We shall not walk into a plague only to encounter what will bring about our destruction." The other pilgrims said: "On the other hand, we shall go, trusting in God; we shall not fight against the decree of God Most High nor shall we flee death, but we will be like those of whom God Most High said: *Consider those of old, who went forth from their habitations in the thousands, facing death* [2:243]." When they turned to ᶜUmar to ask his advice, he said: "Let us return and not walk into a plague." Those who opposed his advice said: "We will be fleeing from the decree of God Most High." Then he told them a parable: "What would you think if one of you had a flock of sheep which descended into a valley with two branches, one fertile and the other arid. If they grazed in the fertile branch would they not be grazing in accordance with the decree of God Most High, and if they grazed in the barren part would they not also be grazing according to the decree of God Most High?" They said: "Indeed." Then he sought ᶜAbd ar-Raḥmān b. Awf to ask his advice, but he was out. When he came the next morning ᶜUmar asked ᶜAbd ar-Raḥmān about it, and he said: "O commander of the faithful, I heard something in that regard from the Messenger of God ﷺ," to which ᶜUmar responded: "God is great!" ᶜAbd ar-Raḥmān said: "I heard the Messenger of God say: 'When you hear of a plague in the land, do not proceed there; but if it should break out in a land where you are, do not flee from it." ᶜUmar—may God be pleased with him—rejoiced at that and praised God Most High for confirming his advice, and returned from Jābiya with his people.[150] So would not all of the companions of the Prophet ﷺ have to concur in renouncing trust in God, which is one of the highest stations, if things like those mentioned were among the conditions of such trust?

Now you might say: why did he forbid fleeing the region afflicted by plague? For the cause of plague is the wind, according to medical science, and the obvious method of treatment is to flee from what is harmful, yet the wind is harmful. So renouncing trust in God in such situations would be permitted, so this example does not prove what you wanted it to. But those who would reject it as objectionable [should know]—though knowledge [of such things] rests with God Most High—that the wind is not harmful insofar as it encounters the body externally but only insofar as one inhales it for a long time. For since there is decay in it and it penetrates to the lungs and the heart, the interior of the intestines is affected by it only after prolonged inhalation, so the plague does not manifest itself externally except after such prolonged internal effects. So leaving the region would not release those already affected from the effects which had taken root beforehand. However, one might imagine oneself to be cured, so we can assimilate this to the class of illusory treatments, like incantations and omens of birds and the like. So if that were all there was to it, then fleeing could not be prohibited. It could only be prohibited were another factor linked to it. Consider: if those who are healthy were permitted to leave so that only the sick who were crippled with illness remained, their hearts would be crushed for they would lack anyone to care for them. No one who could give them water to drink or food to eat would have remained in the country, and they would be unable to take up that task themselves, so the effect would be their total annihilation. [And so far as the others are concerned], one could hope for their cure as one might hope for a cure of the healthy, for if they were to stay, their staying need not mean certain death, nor if they were to leave would their leaving unequivocally spell their release, yet it would certainly mean the destruction of those who stayed.

Muslims are like a building with one part supporting another, so the faithful are like a single body: when a complaint comes from one member it is communicated to the others.[151] This is what we can offer in explanation of the prohibition [of fleeing from a plague-ridden place]. It is quite otherwise with those who have not yet reached the place itself, for the wind has not affected their organs nor do the people of the country need them. Indeed, if the only ones remaining in the place were those stricken by plague, and they were in need of people to help them, and some people came to them, then perhaps it would be [309] preferable to go in to help them. It is not prohibited for one to enter in order to counter the harm, supposing there is hope of alleviating the harm to those Muslims remaining. This shows why fleeing from the plague is likened in some traditions to fleeing in the face of an advancing army,[152] since that action disheartens the Muslims left behind, and so contributes to their destruction. These are delicate matters, so whoever does not ponder them but looks only to the literal meaning of the reports and traditions, will find many contradictions in what he hears. In fact, the servants [of God] and ascetics made many errors in this domain, so knowledge and the benefits flowing from it are especially noteworthy here.

Now you might say: there is indeed benefit in renouncing treatment, as you have noted, but why didn't the Messenger of God ﷺ renounce them to gain these benefits? We would say: in this matter, the benefit is linked to the extent of one's sinfulness and one's need to atone for it. Or to one's fear for oneself that good health could master him or passions overcome him; or to the need to recall one's death in order to overcome heedlessness, or to one's need to gain the reward of patience, given that he falls short of the stations of those who are perfectly content and trusting in God. Or it may be that his inner vision falls short of penetrating to the subtler benefits which God Most High has placed in treatments, so that in his case it all appears illusory, like incantations; or perhaps he is so occupied with his condition as to keep him from treatment, or that treatments distract him from his condition, given his inability to consider the entire situation. One may trace the various responses to renouncing treatment to one of these scenarios. And all of them may be perfections with regard to the rank of the Messenger of God ﷺ whose station is higher than all those stations, since his state requires that his spiritual vision function in the same manner, whether means be at issue or not, for the insight he has into states is like that of the One who makes causes to be causes. Means can do no harm to one who dwells in this station. Just as longing for goods is a weakness, so an aversion to goods as distasteful—though it may be a perfection—is nonetheless a weakness relative to someone who is indifferent to goods being present or absent. Regarding stone or gold as equal is more perfect than fleeing from gold and not stone, and the state of the Prophet—may God's blessing and peace be upon him—was such that mud or gold were equal in his eyes. If he did not keep any, it was to teach creatures the station of renunciation, which marks [for most] the limit of their power, and not for any fear of himself in keeping it. For his rank was too high a rank for [anything in] the world to alter; indeed the treasures of the earth were offered to him yet he declined to take them.

In the same way, using means or renouncing them was indifferent to him, given his spiritual vision, so he would not forego having recourse to treatment in accordance with the *sunna* of God Most High, thereby letting his community feel their need—especially since there is no harm in having recourse to treatment, by contrast with storing up possessions, which is very harmful. Indeed, having recourse to treatment is only harmful when one believes the treatment to be useful apart from the creator of the treatment—which is prohibited; or when one seeks health by treatments to facilitate sinning—and that is prohibited as well. But the faithful in most cases do not intend anything like that, nor do any of the faithful regard treatments as useful in their own right, but only insofar as God Most High makes them useful means, much as one does not regard water as quenching [thirst] or bread as satiating [hunger—outside of the role they play in the *sunna* of God]. For the ordering of treatment to its goal is like the ordering of "acquired action"[*kasb*].[153] For if the acquired action be oriented to having recourse to prescribed actions or to sinful ones, that was indeed its ordering; but if the acquired action was oriented to enjoying what is permissible, then that is its ordering. It should be clear from the various meanings which we have expounded that renouncing treatment can be more beneficial in some states, and having recourse to them more beneficial in others, and that will differ according to the diverse states, individuals, and intentions. So neither acting nor foregoing [as such] is a condition of trusting in God—except for dispensing with illusory means like cauterizing or sorcery, for those are mired in arrangements not befitting those who trust in God.

[3.43] *Explaining the states of those who trust in God with regard to disclosing or concealing illness*

You should understand that concealing sickness, hiding penury and other sorts of trials, belongs to the treasury of piety and is one of the highest stations.[154] For complete contentment [*riḍā'*] with the disposition of God, and patience in the face of his trials, is a form of intercourse between the servant and God—Great and Glorious—so that concealing such things can secure one from harm. [310] Nonetheless, there is no objection to disclosure when one's intention and objective are authentic. The objectives of disclosure are of three sorts. First, when one intends to have recourse to treatment and needs to mention it to the doctor, yet speaks [of his situation] not by way of complaint but by an account which displays how the decree of God Most High has affected him. This was how Bishr [b. al-Ḥārith al-Ḥāfī] described his illness to ᶜAbd ar-Raḥmān the physician, and how Aḥmad b. Ḥanbal related the illness visited upon him, saying: Let me describe the decree of God Most High in my regard."[155] Second, that one describes it not to a physician but to one whom one wishes to emulate, who is rooted in spiritual understanding [*maᶜrifa*]. So by mentioning it one wants to learn from him the appropriate attitude of patience with regard to illness, not to say a right attitude of gratitude to show that he sees the illness to be a blessing for which he will give thanks. So he will speak of it as one speaks of good fortune. Ḥasan al-Baṣrī said: "When a sick person praises God Most High and thanks him, then speaking of his illness will not be a complaint."[156]

Third, that one might thereby manifest one's weakness and need to God Most High. For that is the proper attitude for one who appears to be strong and courageous, and for whom weakness seems unlikely. As it is related of ᶜAlī—may God be pleased with him—when someone asked him in the midst of his illness: "How are you?" he answered: "Terrible," and they looked at one another as though offended by what he said, taking it to be a complaint. So he continued: "I am quite resigned to God," yet he preferred to show his weakness and need, given that one knew him to be strong and hardy.[157] In that he let himself be guided by the practice of the Prophet—may God's blessing and peace be upon him: when ᶜAlī—may God look kindly on his face—was sick and he heard about him saying: "O God, give me patience in the face of affliction," [the Prophet ﷺ] said to him: "You have asked God Most High for affliction; ask God for good health!"[158]

So long as these are one's intentions, it is permissible to mention one's illness, on the sole condition that mentioning it does not amount to a complaint. For complaining of God Most High is prohibited, just as begging on the part of poor people is mentioned among prohibited things—except in the case of dire need. For making a complaint can be associated with exasperation and with showing contempt for the action of God Most High. But if it is free from any association of exasperation and proceeds from the intentions which we have noted, [speaking of one's illness] is not listed among prohibited things. Nevertheless, it has been determined that it is better to forego speaking of it, perhaps because of an [inevitable] hint of complaint, or that there may be fabrication or exaggeration in describing the onset of illness; while for those who renounce treatment as a way of trusting in God, there is no reason at all in their case to manifest it. Yet on balance it is certainly more beneficial to refresh oneself by treatment than to broadcast [one's plight]![159] One of them has said: "Whoever broadcasts [his plight] has no patience." And another has commented on His [having Jacob] say [in the Qur'an]: *sweet patience* [12:18, 83], that is to say: it has no complaint in it.[160] When Jacob—peace be upon him—was asked: "What took away your sight?" he answered: "The bitterness of time and a long sadness!" So God Most High suggested to him: "You have given yourself over to complaining to My servants," to which he responded: "O Lord, I will turn to you in repentance."[161] It is told that Ṭāwūs [b. Kaysān al-Hawlānī] and Mujāhid [b. Jabr al-Makkī] said: "It will be written of a sick man that his sighing was a provocation."[162] They held the sighing of a sick person in contempt because it displays a sense of complaining. So it is said: "All that Iblis achieved in the way of cursing God from Job—peace be upon him—was his sighing in his affliction, and as a result sighing was determined as [Iblis'] lot."[163]

In a report it says: "When a servant is sick, God inspires two angels: 'Make clear what he is to say to one who visits him—to praise God and commend what is good, asking it for him'; and should someone complain or speak in a derogatory manner, say [to him]: 'you will be like that'."[164] So it is that some servants hate to have visitors [when they are sick], for fear that they will complain or exaggerate in their speech. So some of them were in the habit of locking the door when they were ill so that no one would come in, until they had recovered and could go out to them. Fuḍayl [b. ʿIyāḍ]. Wahab [b. al-Ward al-Makkī], and Bisr [b. al-Hārit al-Hāfī] were among these, and Fuḍayl said: "My wish when I am ill is that I shall have no visitors." He also said: "I hate illness only on account of the visitors!"[165] May God be pleased with him and with all of them!

This is the Book of Faith in Divine Unity [*tawḥīd]* and of Trust in Divine Providence [*tawakkul*], by the help of God, and the attitudes conforming to it. God Most High willing, it will be followed by the Book of Love, of Ardent Desire, of Intimacy and of Perfect Contentment—with God blessing it and the Most High confirming.[166]

Notes

1. An allusion, perhaps, to Socrates' mixed praise of the practice of the Athenian analogues to attorneys, the sophists.

2. The analogue of "laws of nature" for Ash'arites is the "customary pattern of action" with which things are imbued by their creator, assimilated to the pattern of action prescribed by Islamic tradition [*sunna*] according to which human beings are promised reward or punishment.

3. A nearly verbatim allusion to 53:23, using 'soul' [*nafs*] in the way Sufis do: an inner compulsion which eludes reason.

4. Makkī, *Qūt al-qulūb* 2, 4:17-18; 4:22-23.

5. Makkī, *Qūt al-qulūb* 2, 4, 30-31 / 3,6.

6. A celebrated image, yet Gramlich notes that what for Ghazālī is the highest stage is the lowest for Sahl at-Tustarī (*Kalām Sahl*, Hs. Köprülü 727, 101b-102a); and also for Qushayrī (*Risāla* 76, 11-13, *bab at-tawakkul*), Anṣārī, *Sharh ar-Risāla al-Qushayrīya* 3, 49, and Suhrawardī, *ᶜAwārif al-maᶜārif*, Kap. 60, 25.

7. "He who contracts," with "He who expands," form a doublet in the classsical ninety-nine names of God—cf. *99 Beautiful Names of God*, 81-2.

8. In the Ash'arite picture of human action to which Ghazālī subscribes and to which he alludes here, the created subject is the locus [*mahal*] of actions created by God, which are thereby performed [*kasb*] by the creature.

9. In the text, an adverbial construction adapted from the divine name, *al-Haqq*—see *99 Beautiful Names*, 129; and for *al-Wakīl*, 126.

10. Abu Hurayra relates this word of the prophet; cf. Munāwī, *Fayd al-qadīr* 3, 108, Nr. 2870; "Azīzī, *As-sirāj al-munīr* 2, 96-97.

11. Munāwī, *Fayd al-qadīr* 6, 189, Nr. 8896; ᶜAzīzī, *As-sirāj al-munīr* 3, 376.

12. See, for example, Ahmad b. Hanbal, *al-musnad*, ed. Halabī, 5, 233; 5, 247.

13. *Al-Wāhid*, *al-Haqq*; cf. *99 Beautiful Names*, 130-31, 124-26.

14. Qushayrī, *Risāla* 76, 7-11. Ghazālī's source for all the Sufi sayings in this section will be Qushayrī.

15. This use of *'bi' l wājib'* is explored by Richard Frank, *Creation....*

16. Related by ʿUmar b. al-Hattāb, Ibn al-Jawzī, *Al-wafā bi-ahwāl al-Mustafā* I, 238.

17. Qushayrī, *Risāla* 77, 6-9.

18. Ibid., 77, 9-12.

19. Ibid., 12-13.

20. Makkī, *Qūt al-qulūb* 1, 229, 31-33 / 2, 140.

21. Qushayrī, *Risāla* 77, 14-15.

22. Ibid., 77, 23-24.

23. Ibid., 77, 34-35.

24. The three categories in Islamic law, with permissible reserved to indifferent actions.

25. Words of Sahl according to Makkī, *Qūt al-qulūb* 2, 19,10-11 / 3,27.

26. Ibid., 2, 197, 3-4 / 4,90.

27. Makkī, *Qūt al-qulūb* 2, 4, 24-26 / 3, 6.

28. Makkī, *Qūt al-qulūb* 2, 4, 24-26 / 3, 6.

29. Makkī, *Qūt al-qulūb* 2, 4, 26-28 / 3, 6.

30. Abbreviated from Makkī, Ibid., 2, 4-5 / 3,6; *al-ʿAzīz* is a name of God (cf. *99 Beautiful Names* 65-66) whose derivation from *ʿaz* [strength] is lost in translation.

31. Ibid., 2, 6,16-17 / 3.8.

32. Ibid., 2, 18, 28-32 /n 3, 35.

33. The sense here seems to be that one can be so attached to the actual money which he has earned that he forgets that coins are a neutral means of exchange.

34. Makkī, *Qūt al-qulūb* 2, 18, 4-7 / 3, 24.

35. The image of "looking up to" reminds one of a beggar at street level pleading with his eyes to passers-by. For the Sufi use of 'soul' here, see note 56.

36. Makkī, *Qūt al-qulūb* 2, 17, 14-17 / 3, 24-25. The presumption must be that his initial turning away was a matter of undue pride in taking anything at all—even something contracted.

37. Ibid., 2, 17, 17-18 / 3, 25.

38. Qushayri, *Risāla* 77, 20-22, *bāb at-tawakkul*.

39. Sarrāj, *Al-luma'* 195, 14-17.

40. Makkī, Ibid. 2, 17, 30-31 / 3, 27.

41. ʿIrāqī, *Al-mughnī* 4, 263.

42. Sarraj, *Al-luma'* 53, reporting Dārānī; somewhat different in Makkī, Ibid. 2, 2, 16-17 / 3,3.

43. Makkī, Ibid. 2, 6, 19 / 3, 8-9.

44. An Arabic saying which foresees that any person who is apprehesive about another will always think the worst; in Freytag, *Arabum Proverbia* 1, 11, Nr. 18.

45. Makkī, Ibid. 2, 15, 1-3 / 3, 21.

46. Ibid.

47. Qushayrī, *Risāla* 80, *bāb at-tawakkul,* ad fin.

48. Qushayrī, *Risāla* 78-79; Anṣārī, *Sharh ar-Risāla* 3, 58-59.

49. Qushayrī, Ibid., 79, 10-12; Anṣarī, Ibid., 3, 59.

50. Ibid., 79, 17-20; 3, 59.

51. Ibid., 79-80; 3, 61.

52. Adapted from Makkī, *Qūt al-qulūb 2, 8, 2-8 / 3, 11.*

53. Qushayrī, *Risāla* 80, 2-15; Anṣārī, *Sharh ar-Risāla* 3, 61-62.

54. Ibid., 78, 35-36; 3, 58.

55. Ibid., 78; 58.

56. A similar account is given by G͟hazālī in *99 Beautiful Names*, to illustrate God as "the Benevolent [*al-Latīf*]," 97.

57. Makkī, *Qūt al-qulūb* 2, 9, 20 / 3, 13.

58. Ibid., 2, 9, 21-22 / 3, 13.

59. Anonymous saying in Makkī, Ibid., 2, 196, 15-16 / 4, 89; with variant at 2, 7, 33 / 3, 11.

60. Qushayrī, *Risāla* 78, 26-28; Anṣārī, *Sharh ar-Risāla 3, 57.*

61. Literally, 'broken', as a horse has to be broken; an appropriate image for the soul as our lower power.

62. Makkī, *Qūt al-qulūb* 2, 29, 6-9 / 3, 29.

63. This commentary on 2:51: "And when we did appoint for Moses forty nights [of solitude], and then you chose the calf, when he had gone from you, and were wrongdoers;" is inspired by Makkī, Ibid., 2, 191, 7-12 / 4, 85-86.

64. ʿIrāqī, *Al-mughnī* 4, 269-70.

65. Makkī, Ibid. 2, 20, 27-32 / 3, 30.

66. Ibid., 2, 20, 11-12 / 3, 29.

67. ʿIrāqī, *Al-mughnī* 4, 271.

68. Ibid.

69. Makkī, Ibid. 2, 21, 17-18 / 3,31.

70. Recourse to branding was a way of seeking assurance outside of God's plan; Ibid. 2, 21, 4-5 / 3, 31.

71. Ibid. 2, 19, 28-35 / 3, 28.

72. A celebrated hadith even in the west; Qushayrī, *Risāla* 76, 19-20, *bāb at-tawakkul;* Anṣārī, *Sharh ar-Risāla* 3, 49.

73. On the "prayer of fear" or prayer when one is in danger of being attacked, see SEI 496b.

74. See Ibn Isḥaq's *Sīrat Rasūl Allah*, translated by A. Guillaume: *The Life of Muhammad* (Oxford: Oxford University Press, 1955) 224.

75. Such stories are legion; see Qushayrī, *Risāla* 166, 13-14; Anṣārī, *Sharh ar-Risāla al-Qushayrīya* 4, 173.

76. ʿIrāqī, *al-mugnī* 4, 263.
77. Makkī, *Qūt al-qulūb* 2, 33, 19 / 3, 48.
78. Ibid. 2, 33, 17-20 / 3, 48.
79. Ibid. 2, 33, 13-16 / 3, 48.
80. Ibid. 2, 33, 5-8 / 3, 48; the words of the Prophet are found in ʿIrāqī, *Al-mughnī* 4, 274.
81. Ibid. 2, 32, 25-29 / 3, 47.
82. Ibid. 2, 33-34 / 3, 49.
83. Ibid. 2, 34, 2-8 / 3, 49.
84. Ibid. 2, 34, 29-33 / 3, 50.
85. Ibid. 2, 34, 18 / 3, 50.
86. Ibid. 2, 34, 8-11 / 3, 49.
87. Ibid. 2, 34, 11-13 / 3, 49-50.
88. Ibid. 2, 34, 18-20 / 3, 50.
89. Ibid. 2, 34, 20-21 / 3, 50; a reminder how retaliation inaugurates a never-ending chain.
90. Ibid. 2, 34, 21-23 / 3, 50.
91. Ibid. 2, 34, 23-24 / 3, 50.
92. Ibid. 2, 34, 24-25 / 3, 50.
93. See Aḥmad b. Ḥanbal, *Al-musnad*, ed. Halabi, 4, 251-52.
94. Makkī, Ibid. 2, 21, 7-9 / 3, 30.
95. Ibid.
96. Ibid. 2, 21, 9-10 / 3, 30.
97. Ibid.
98. Ibid. 2, 21, 10-11 / 3, 30.
99. Ibid. 2, 21, 15-16 / 3, 31.
100. Citations in Wensinck, *Concordance* 5, 547b, 54-55.
101. Makkī, Ibid. 2, 21, 20-21 / 3, 31.
102. Ibid. 2, 21, 21-22/ 3, 31.
103. Ibn Māja, *Sunan* 2, 1139, Nr. 3443, ṭibb 3.
104. Makkī, Ibid.
105. Ibid. 2, 21, 23 / 3, 31.
106. Ibn Māja, *Sunan* 2, 1158, Nr 3502.
107. Two older works with the title *Tibb an-nabī* are known, one by Ibn as-Sunni and another by Abū Nu'aym al-Iṣfahānī.
108. Makkī, Ibid. 2, 21, 31-36 / 3, 31.
109. Ibid. 2, 22, 1-2 / 3, 31-32.
110. The terms used here—*hikma* [wisdom], *hakam* [authority]—are variants of a name of God: *al-Hakam*—the Arbitrator; see G͟hazālī's treatment of that name in *99 Beautiful Names*, 85-92.
111. Cf. Ormsby, *Theodicy in Islamic Thought*..
112. Makkī, Ibid. 2, 22, 30-31 / 3, 33.
113. See Buhārī, *Sahīh*, ṭibb 37.
114. Makkī, Ibid. 2, 22, 32-36 / 3, 33.
115. Ibid. 2, 23, 2-3 / 3, 33.

116. Ibid. 2, 23, 3-4 / 3, 33.

117. Ibid 2, 23, 4-6 / 3, 33.

118. Ibid. 2, 23, 7-9 / 3, 33. The Qur'anic verse makes reference to ancient inhabitants of the Hejaz, the ruins of whose dwellings were presented as poignant reminders to the Arabs of kingdoms now defunct.

119. Ibid. 22, 22, 31-32 / 3, 33.

120. Ibid. 2, 23, 6-7 / 3, 33; also 2, 16, 25-26 / 3, 23-24.

121. *Al-Hayy, al-Qayyūm* are two names of God often invoked in tandem; see *99 Beautiful Names*, 129-30.

122. Makkī, Ibid. 2, 24-25 / 3, 36.

123. Ibid. 2, 25, 1-2 / 3, 36.

124. Ibid. 2, 25, 2-3 / 3, 36.

125. Ibid. 2, 24, 1 / 3, 34.

126. Ibid. 2, 23, 35-36 / 3, 34.

127. *Al-Haqq* is the divine name favored among Sufis; see *99 Beautiful Names*, 124-26.

128. Makkī, Ibid. 2, 25, 10-11 / 3, 36.

129. Ibid. 2, 25, 6-8 / 3, 36; the same verb—*krh*—can mean 'coerce' and 'hate'.

130. Ibid. 2, 23, 22-28 / 3, 34.

131. Ibid. 2, 24, 17-18 / 3, 35.

132. Ibid.

133. Ibid. 2, 24, 19-20 / 3, 35.

134. Ibid., 2, 24, 20-22 / 3, 35. On the Anṣari, see EI 1:514.

135. Ibid. 2, 24, 25-26 / 3, 35.

136. Ibid 2, 24, 29-30 / 3, 35-36.

137. Ibid. 2, 24, 1-2 / 3, 34.

138. Ibid 2, 24, 5 / 3, 35.

139. Ibid. 2, 24, 7-8 / 3, 35.

140. Ibid. 2, 24, 8-10 / 3, 35.

141. Ibid. 2, 24, 11-13 / 3, 35.

142. Ibid. 2, 26, 14 / 3, 38.

143. Ibid. 2, 26, 15 / 3, 38.

144. Ibid. 2, 26, 16-17 / 3, 38.

145. Ibid. 2, 26, 17-19 / 3, 38.

146. Ibid. 2, 26, 19-21 / 3, 38.

147. Ibid. 2, 26, 21-23 / 3, 38.

148. Ibid. 2, 26, 23 / 3, 38.

149. Ibid. 2, 26, 23-25 / 3, 38.

150. Ibid. 2, 26, 26-27,2 / 3, 38-39.

151. These two images are taken from hadiths: Wensinck, *Concordance* 1, 223a; *Sahīh* 4, 1999-2000, birr 66.

152. Ahmad b. Ḥanbal, *Al-musnad*, ed. Ḥalabī, 6, 82.

153. For an extended discussion of *kasb*, see my *Freedom and Creation in Three Traditions* (Notre Dame IN: University of Notre Dame Press, 1993); see also Richard Frank's suggestion that this expression be translated 'performance', in his "Moral Obligation in Classical Muslim Theology," *Journal of Religious Ethics* 11 (1983) 204-223, esp. note 19.

154. Hadith according to Anas b. Mālik in Munāwī, *Fayd al-qadīr* 3, 294-95 Nr. 3439.

155. Makkī, Ibid. 2, 28, 33-34 / 3, 42.

156. Ibid.

157. Ibid. 2, 28-29 / 3, 42.

158. Ibid. 2, 29, 2-4 / 3, 42.

159. Ibid. 2, 28, 17-20 / 3, 41.

160. Ibid. 2, 28, 20 / 3, 41.

161. Ibid. 2, 28, 20-22 / 3, 41.

162. Ibid.

163. Ibid. 2, 28, 23-24 / 3, 41.

164. [cf Gramlich E 234]

165. Ibid. 2, 28, 28 / 3, 41.

166. Marie Louis Siauve's translation of *Kitāb al-ḥubb* of the *Iḥyā'* is entitled *Livre de l'amour* (Paris: Vrin, 1986)

APPENDIX

Persons Cited in Text
(Excluding prophets)

[ʿABDULLĀH] IBN ʿUMAR—see IBN ʿUMAR

ʿABD AL-RAḤMĀN ibn Abī Bakr al-Qurashī (d. c 54 [673/4]) The elder son of Abū Bakr, he participated in his father's campaign in the Yamāma, where he acquired some fame as an archer. (*Isaba*, II.399 40I; *Istīʿāb*, II.391-4.)

ʿABD AL-RAḤMĀN IBN ʿAWF al-Qurashī (d. 31 [652]) One of the first to respond to the Prophet's call in Mecca, he took part in the migration to Abyssinia. A wealthy merchant, he donated huge sums in charity, and was one of the council of six nominated by ʿUmar to choose his successor, as well as being one of the ten men assured of Heaven by the Prophet while they still lived. (EI2, 1. 84 [M.Th. Houtsma—W. Montgomery Watt]; *Isaba*, 11.408-10.)

ABŪ ʿABD AL-RAḤMĀN Possibly Muhammad ibn al-Ḥusayn ibn Muḥammad al-Azdī al-Sulamī al-Nīsābūrī (d. 412 [1021]), who was a writer, historian, and Sufi sheikh and also one of the teachers of al-Quṣhayrī. Transmitted traditions from ʿUmar, Uthman, ʿAlī, Abū'l-Darda, and others. (Qushayrī [1988], intro. p. 9; Abū Nuʿaym IV.192.)

ABU ʿALĪ al-Ḥasan ibn ʿAlī al-Nīsābūrī "AL-DAQQĀQ" The teacher, sheikh and father in law of al-Qushayrī, who makes more references to him than to anyone else in his famous *Risāla*. Al-Qushayrī married his daughter, Fātima, who was a learned *ḥadīth* transmitter in her own right, and, when al-Qushayrī died in 465 (hijra), he was buried alongside of his teacher. (Qushayrī [1988], intro. pp. 7-9)

ABŪ ᶜALĪ AL-RŪDHBĀRĪ Aḥmad ibn Muḥammad ibn al-Qasim (d. 322 [933/4]) A well known Sufi sheikh in Egypt, originally from Baghdad. He was associated with the circle of al-Junayd, al-Nūrī, and Abū Hamza. Well known for his deep understanding of the mystical way (*tarīqa*), he was also a *ḥadīth* scholar and a jurist who studied under Ibrahīm Harbī. (Abu Nuᶜaym, 1.185-6; Sulamī, 362-9; Sulamī [1986] 354-60; *Tarīkh Baghdād*, I.329 33.)

ABŪ ᶜABDULLĀH [Muḥammad Ibn Said] AL-QURASHI A Sufi sheikh who is cited twice by al-Qushayri and who apparently wrote a dogmatic treatise elucidating faith in divine unity: *Sharh al-Tawhīd.* (Qushayrī [1988], 165, 321; Abū Nuᶜaym X.337, 338).

ABŪ BAKR AL-ṢIDDĪQ (d. 13 [634]) Disputably the closest Companion and chief advisor of the Prophet, he became the first recognized "Deputy" of the Prophet following the latter's death in 10/632. He accompanied Muhammad on his flight to al-Medina in 622, and was chosen to lead congregational prayers during the Prophet's final illness. When he himself passed away two years later, he was buried alongside the Prophet. (El2, 1. 113-4 [W. M. Watt] .)

ABŪ BAKR AL-MARWAZĪ Unidentified.

ABU'L-DARDĀ', ᶜUwaymir al-Khazrajī (d. 32 [652/3]) A celebrated Companion of the Prophet who joined Islam sometime after the battle of Badr, whereupon he is said to have given up commerce in order to occupy himself with worship with the *ahl al-Suffa*. He was one of those who gathered together the text of the Qur'an during the Prophet's lifetime. He died in Damascus, where he was buried, and is venerated in particular by the Sufis (EI2, I. II3-4 [A. Jeffery]; Abū Nuᶜaym, I. 208-27.)

ABŪ DHARR, Jundub ibn Junāda al-Ghifārī (d. c. 32[652/3]) One of the earliest Muslims, his shyness and devout temperament made him the protagonist of a rich variety of legendary material. He also transmitted a large number of Traditions: al-Bukhārī and Muslim between them include thirty-one of these. (EI2, 1. 114-5 [J. Robson]; Massignon, *Essai*, 158-9; *Istīʿāb*, IV. 62-5.)

ABŪ HAMZA AL-KHURASANĪ Originally from Nishapur, he was a contemporary of Junayd and a travelling companion of Abū Turāb al-Nakhshabī and Abū Saʿīd al-Kharrāz. He is said to have been one of the youngest sheikhs as well as one of the most pious. (Sulamī [1986] 326-8.)

ABŪ HURAYRA al-Dawsī al-Yamānī (d. c. 58 [677/8]) One of the most copious narrators of Tradition, and also a model of poverty and the fear of God's chastisement. He is said to have joined Islam during the Khaybar expedition (7/629); after which he became one of the *ahl al-Suffa*. After the Prophet's death he was appointed governor of Bahrayn by ʿUmar. (Azami, 35-7. EI2,1.I29 [J. Robson]; *Isaba*, IV.200-8.)

ABŪ JA'FAR AL-ḤADDĀD Associate of Abū Turāb and one of the most notable Muslims of his time. An early ascetic, it is said that for twenty years he lived by working for a dinar a day, spending it on the poor while fasting himself. Between dusk and night prayer, he would leave the mosque to share his meager fare with the needy. Sheikh of al-Junayd, he was known for his strength in *ijtihād* and widely respected as a transmitter of traditions. (Sulamī [1986] 234.)

ABŪ MŪSĀ AL-DAYBULĪ Initial transmitter of many traditions from Abū Yazīd. (Sulamī [1986] 68, 73.)

ABŪ SA'ĪD AL-KHARRĀZ, Ahmad ibn ʿIsā (d. 277 [890/ I]) An important Sufi who, according to Hujwīrī, was 'the first to explain the doctrine of annihilation (*fana'*) and subsistence (*baqa'*). He was a close companion of Dhū'l-Nūn, Bishr al-Ḥāfī, and al-Sarī al-Saqaṭī, and was renowned for the emphasis he placed on *ʿishq*, the passionate love of God, and upon the scrupulous observance of the Law. (Sulamī, 223-8; Hujwīrī, 143; Quṣhayrī, 1.161-2; GAS, I.646.)

ABŪ SULAYMĀN AL-DĀRĀNĪ, ʿAbd al-Raḥmān (d. 205 [820/1] or 215 [830/1]) Well-known to the Sufis for his piety and renunciation, he was responsible for characteristic maxims such as "The heart is ruined when fear departs from it even for one moment," and "The sign of perdition is the drying up of tears." (Qushayrī, 1. 108-10; Sulamī, 68-73; Hujwīrī, 112-3; Abū Nuʿaym, IX.254-80.)

ABŪ ṬĀLIB AL-MAKKĪ, ibn Muḥammad ibn ʿAṭīya al-Hārithī (d. 386 [996/7]) A famous Sufi and traditionist, leader of the dogmatic school of the Sālimīya in Basra. His chief work is the *Qūt al-qulūb*, which was studied closely by Ghazālī. (Ibn Khallikān, III.20-2I; EI2, 1.153 [L. Massignon].)

['Askar Ibn Hasīn] ABŪ TURĀB AN-NAKHSHABĪ (d. 245) Associate of Abū Khatim al-'Aṭṭar al-Baṣrī, and also of al-Aṣamm al-Balkhī, one of the greatest sheikhs of Khurāsān, widely respected for knowledge, legal decisions, trust in God (*al-tawakkul*), asceticism, and piety. Died in the desert, where "it is said that a lion ripped him to pieces." (Sulamī [1986], 146-51, Abū Nuʿaym X.45-51 [462].)

ABŪ UMĀMA AL-BĀHILĪ, Ṣudayy ibn ʿAjlān (d. 81 [700/1] or 86 [705/6]) A companion of the Prophet who related a large number of Traditions. He was sent to certain of the desert tribes, and won many converts with the aid of miracles. He later removed to Homs; according to Ibn ᶜUyayna he was the last Companion of the Prophet to die in Syria. (*Isāba*, 11. 175-6; *Istīᶜāb*, IV.4; *Mashāhīr*, 50.)

ABŪ YA'QŪB AL-AQTĀ' AL-BAṢRĪ Unidentified.

ABŪ YA'QŪB AL-ṢŪṢĪ Mentioned as a contemporary of al-Junayd; a Sufi sheikh and transmitter of *aḥādīth*. (Sulamī, 378.)

ABŪ YAZĪD Tayfūr b. ᶜIsā b. Surūshan AL-BISTĀMĪ (d. 261 [874] or 264 [877-8]) One of the most celebrated of Sufi mystics, with some five hundred sayings passed down, many of which express near-identification with God. Theopathic exclamations, such as "Glory be to me!" and "How great is My majesty!" tended to garner the hostility of orthodox theologians. He may have been influenced by Indian sources through his teacher Abu ᶜAlī al-Sindi. (EI2, 1.162-3 [H. Ritter].)

AḤMAD IBN ABI'L-ḤAWĀRĪ, Abu'l-Ḥasan (d. c 230 [844/ 5]) An early Syrian exponent of Sufism, a disciple of al-Dārānī and a companion of Ibn ᶜUyayna. He is said to have thrown away his books and lived the life of a wandering ascetic. (Hujwīrī, 118 9; Qushayrī, 1.117; Sulamī, 88, 92.)

AḤMAD IBN ḤANBAL (d. 24I [855]) The great *ḥadīth* scholar after whom the Ḥanbalī school of law is named. He travelled extensively in search of Traditions, of which he is said to have committed over three hundred thousand to memory. A companion of Bis͟hr al-Hāfī and Ma'rūf al-Karkhī, he was held in high regard by the Sufis, who attribute a number of miracles to him. His tomb became one of the most frequented centres of pilgrimage in Baghdad; indeed, Hallāj himself was known to pray there. (EI2, 1. 272-7 [H. Laoust]; Abū Nuᶜaym, IX.I6I-234; Hujwīrī, 117-8.)

[ABŪ SA'ĪD] AḤMAD IBN ʿĪSĀ AL-KHARRĀZ (d. 279) Associate of Dhū'l-Nūn al-Miṣrī, Abū Abdullāh al-Mibājī, Abū ʿUbayd al-Baṣrī; said to be among the greatest of the sheikhs of his time and the first to speak of *fanā* and *baqā*; a respected transmitter of *aḥādīth*. (Sulamī [1986], 228-32.)

ʿĀ'ISHA bint Abī Bakr (d. 58 [678]) The most beloved wife of the Prophet. During his final illness he asked his other wives for leave to stay in her house, where he died. After his death she was involved in the revolt of Talha and al-Zubayr against the caliph ʿAlī, after which she lived quietly at Medina until she died. She was well-versed in Arab history and in poetry, and some of her verses have been preserved. In addition, she was a tremendously rich source in the transmission of Prophetic Traditions. (EI2, I. 307-8 [W. Montgomery Watt].)

ʿALĪ ibn Abī Ṭālib (d. 40 [661]) First cousin and son-in-law of the Prophet and fourth of the "rightly guided" caliphs, ʿAlī was indisputably one of the closest and most gifted of the Companions in spiritual and religious matters, including exegesis. Most Sufi *silsilāt* are traced back to the Prophet through him. While trying to negotiate a peaceful end to a crucial battle with Mu'āwiya, he lost sovereignty over Syria and later was assassinated. According to the Shī'ī school of thought, he was the first to hold the spiritual office of the *Imama*, which provides spiritual guidance through inspired interpretation of the revelation, which ended with the Prophet Muhammad. (EI2, 1.381-6 [H.A.R. Gibb].)

ʿALĪ IBN AL-FUḌAYL [IBN ʿIYĀḌ] The son of al-Fudayl Ibn ʿIyād, who was a prominent *ḥadīth* transmitter and teacher from Khurāsān. He himself lived in perpetual expectation of the day of judgment: "If I thought I should remain until the afternoon, it would be unbearable for me." (Abū Nuʿaym, VIII. 272, 299.)

ʿAMMAR IBN YASĪR ibn ʿAmīr ibn Mālik (d. 37 [657]) An early convert to Islam and companion of the Prophet, he was renowned for his great piety and considered to have an excellent knowledge of the Traditions of the Prophet. (EI2, 1.448 [H. Reckendorf].)

ANAS ibn Mālik ibn al-Naḍr (d. 91-3 [709/10-711/2]) A celebrated Companion of the Prophet, he had been presented to the Prophet by his mother at an early age in fulfilment of a vow. After the Prophet's death he participated in the wars of conquest. One hundred and twenty eight Traditions on his authority are to be found in the collections of al-Bukhārī and Muslim. (*Isāba*, 1. 84-5; EI2, 1. 482 [A. J. Wensinck— J. Robson].)

AYMAN [IBN ʿUBAYD] Also known as Ibn ʿAliyyah from Yūnis; a transmitter of *aḥādīth*. (Abu Nuʿaym, IV.90.)

AL-BA'ADĪ Unidentified.

BISHR IBN AL-ḤARĪTH "al-Ḥāfī" (d c 227[841/2]) One of the most celebrated figures of early Sufism, he was a companion of Fudayl ibn ʿIyāḍ. Formerly given to riotous living, his repentance is said to have come when, in a state of inebriation he picked up a scrap of paper on which was written the name of God, which he perfumed and put in a clean place. That night he received a dream in which God told him that He would perfume his name as a reward for his act. Many other tales of his charismatic and devout life have found their way into the classical works on Sufism. (Qushayrī, 1. 84-8; Hujwīrī, 105-6; *Siyar*, x.469; Abu Nuʿaym, VIII. 336-60; Sulamī, 33-40; EI2, I. 1244-6 [F. Meier]; Dermenghem, 67—78.)

BUNĀN Ibn Muḥammad AL-ḤAMMĀL (d. 316 [...]) Also known by his kunya, Abu'l-Ḥasan, he lived in Egypt, and was respected as one of the greatest of sheikhs, "who spoke the truth, urging people to the good (*al-maʿrūf*)." His attainment of exalted stations was well-attested, as were the signs attributed to him. An associate of Abū Qasim, Junayd Ibn-Muhammad, and teacher of Abu'l Hussain, he also transmitted *aḥādīth*. Speaking of the seven stations of obedience, he asserted that God created seven heavens, associating each with a degree of obedience: fear and hope, love and grief, loving kindness and timidity, longing and awe, intimate communication and exaltation, divine appointment and magnification, loving kindness and proximity. (Sulamī [1986] 291-94.)

DHU'L-NŪN al-Miṣrī, Thawbān (d. 245 [859/60]) Born in Upper Egypt, he travelled to Mecca and Damascus, and became a leading exponent of Sufism. It is said that he was the first to give a systematic explanation of the *ahwal* ('states') and *maqamat* ('stations') encountered on the spiritual path. A number of miracles are attributed to him, as well as some fine poetry. (E12, 2.242 [M. Smith]; Sulamī, 23-32; Qushayrī, 1. 67-70; Hujwīrī, I00-3; Massignon, *Essai*, 206-I3.)

FATH AL-MAWSILĪ Unidentified.

FUḌAYL IBN ʿIYĀḌ (d. I87 [803/4]) A converted highway robber and a famous ascetic. He studied Tradition under Sufyan al-Thawn at Kufa. The Caliph Harun al-Rashīd called him 'the Prince of the Muslims'. Among the statements attributed to him: "Three traits harden the heart: much food, much sleep, and much speech," and "the beginning of asceticism is contenting oneself with [the decree of] Allah, be he exalted." (EI2, 2.936 [M. Smith], Sulamī [1986] 6-14..)

HAMDŪN AL-QASSĀR (d. 271/884) A celebrated Sufi and learned religious teacher who lived and taught at Nishapur, advising contentment with little and tolerance of others. (EI2, 3.132 [Margaret Smith].)

AL-ḤASAN al-Baṣrī (d. 110 [728/9]) Perhaps the best known personality among the second generation of Muslims, he was born in Medina and took part in the conquest of eastern Iran. He then moved to Baṣra, where his sanctity and great eloquence attracted great numbers to his circle. He was also a judge and an authority on *ḥadith*. His tomb at Baṣra remains an important centre for devout visits. (Hujwīrī, 86-7; Abu Nuᶜaym, I.131-61; Attar, I9-26; EI2, 3.247-8 [H. Ritter].)

ḤU<u>DH</u>AYFA ibn al-Yamān al-'Abasī (d. 36[656/7]) One of the earliest converts to Islam, whose father was martyred at the battle of Uhud. He is particularly revered by the Sufis. He related a considerable number of *ahādīth*, particularly those relating to eschatology: according to the sources he said that "the Prophet told me all that would occur from the present until the Day of Judgement." (*Isaba*, I.3I6-7; Massignon, *Essay*, 109-10; Nawawī, *Tahdhīb*, 199 201; Abu Nuᶜaym, I.270-83.)

ḤU<u>DH</u>AYFA [IBN QATADA] AL-MARASHĪ Mentioned in the report of Khalaf ibn Tamīm: "I have seen five [individuals] the likes of whom I have never seen [before or after]: Ibrāhīm ibn Adhām, Yūsuf ibn Asbāt, Hudhayfa ibn Qatāda, Hushaym al-ᶜIjlī, and Abū Yūnus al-Qawī." (Sulami [1986], 37).

AL-ḤUSAYN AL-MAGHAZILĪ Probably Abū Aḥmad, a contemporary of Junayd and al-Nūrī and an associate of Sarī al-Saqatī and of Sumnūn ibn Hamza (d. 290/930), whose collected utterances focus on love for the divine (*al-mahabba*). (Qushayrī [1988] 407, 439.)

AL-ḤUSAYN IBN MANṢŪR [AL-ḤALLĀJ] (244-309/857-922) The mystical theologian whose life, teaching, and death throw light on a crucial period of Muslim history (tenth-century Baghdad), and whose public disclosures of intimacy with the Divine branded him a heretic and won him imprisonment, torture, and public hanging on a gibbet. His teaching on unity with God through love has been explored in itself and in its consequences by Louis Massignon in his *Passion of al-Hallaj.* (EI2 3.99-104 [L. Massignon, L. Gardet].)

IBN ᶜABBĀS, ᶜAbd Allāh (d. 68 [687/8]) A cousin of the Prophet. He was one of the great scholars, particularly as a Qur'an exegete, of the earliest period of Islam. (EI2, 1. 401 [L. Veccia Vaglieri].)

IBN MAS'ŪD, ᶜAbd Allāh al-Hudhall (d.32-3[652/3-653/4]) Of Bedouin origin, Ibn Mas'ūd is said to have been either the third or the sixth convert to Islam; he became one of the most erudite Companions. He was particularly well versed in the recitation and interpretation of the Qur'an, and was an expert in matters of law. In addition, he related a number of the most important eschatological *ahādīth.* (EI2, 3. 873-5 [J.-C. Vadet]; *Isaba*, II. 360-62; *Istīᶜāb*, II.308-I6.)

IBN ᶜUMAR, ᶜAbd Allāh (d. 73 [693/4]) A Companion of the Prophet who, at the age of fourteen asked to be permitted to fight at Uḥud, which permission was denied. Possessed of high moral qualities he commanded universal deference and respect. Although it is said that he was offered the caliphate on three separate occasions he kept himself aloof from politics and occupied himself instead with study and instruction. (EI2, 1.53-4 [L. Vecchia Vagliere]; *Isāba,* II.338-41; Abū Nuᶜaym, I.292-314.)

IBRĀHĪM IBN ADHAM, Abū Isḥāq ibn Manṣūr ibn Yazīd (d. c I60 [776/7]) A famous ascetic from Balkh. His dramatic conversion, reminiscent of that of Buddha, is well known. (SEI, I55-6 [R.A. Nicholson]; Qushayrī 1 21-23; Hujwīrī, I03-5)

[IBRĀHĪM ibn Aḥmad ibn Isma^cīl] AL-KHAWASS (d. 291) An associate of Junayd and Nuri, he was best known for his explications of the many stages of itinerant wayfaring (*siyāha*) and acsetic discipline (*riyāda*), he was among "the foremost of those wayfaring on the path of *tawakkul*." Many spiritual maxims are attributed to him, such as "he for whom the world does not weep, heaven will not laugh for him." (Sulamī [1986], 284-287)

ᶜIMRĀN IBN ḤASIN Transmitter of *aḥādīth*. (Sulamī II, 42, 78, ...)

AL-JUNAYD, Abu'l-Qāsim ibn Muḥammad (d. 298 [910-11]) One of the best known of the "sober" Sufis of Baghdad and contemporary of al-Hallaj, he stressed the primacy of the station of *baqā'* over *fanā'*. A nephew and disciple of al-Sarl al-Saqatī, he vowed that he would not teach during the latter's lifetime out of deference to his preceptor; however he received a vision of the Prophet, who told him that 'God shall make your words the salvation of a multitude of mankind'; he then began to teach. His gatherings 'were attended by jurists and philosophers (attracted by his precise reasoning), theologians (drawn by his orthodoxy) and Sufis (for his discoursing upon the Truth)'. In addition, he was an authority on theology and law, in which he followed the school of Abū Thawr. (Sulamī, 141-50; GAS, I. 647-50; EI2, 2.600 [A.J. Arberry]; A. H. Abdel-Kader, *The Life, Personality and Writings of al-Junayd*.)

MĀLIK IBN DĪNĀR al-Nājī (d. 131 [748/9]) An ascetic of Basra who made a living by copying the Qur'an. A companion of al-Ḥasan al-Baṣrī, he was credited with a number of miracles, including the ability to walk on water.

(*Mashahīr*, 90; Hujwīrī, 89 90; *Ghaya*, II.36; Abu Nuᶜaym, II. 357-88.)

MAMSHADH AL-DINAWARĪ (d. 299) Esteemed by Sulamī as one of the greatest sheikhs of his time, he was known for his extensive mystical knowledge and deep understanding. Many utterances are related from him, including, "to the gnostic belongs a mirror; when he looks into it, His Lord reveals Himself to him." (Sulamī [1986] 316-17.)

AL-MUGHĪRA IBN SHU'BA al-Thaqafī (d. 50 [670/1]) A Companion of the Prophet. He took part in a number of the early conquests, and lost an eye at the battle of Yarmuk. The caliph ᶜUmar made him governor of Basra and then of Kufa; he subsequently retired from politics until it became clear that Muᶜāwiya had won, when he again assumed the governorship of the latter city. (*Isaba*, 111.432-3.)

MUJĀHID ibn Jabr al-Makkī (d. 104 [722/3]) Sometimes considered the most learned authority among the 'Followers' (*al-tābᶜūn*) in the exegesis of the Qur'an, which he learned from Ibn ᶜAbbās, he was particularly concerned with the circumstances under which each verse had been revealed. He was also respected for his austere and pious lifestyle. (*Mashahīr*, 82; *Fihrist*, 33; *Ghaya*, II. 41-2; Abu Nuᶜaym, III.)

MUTARRIF IBN ᶜABD ALLĀH IBN AL-SHIKHKHĪR al-Amirī (d. c 87 [806/7]) An ascetic and a traditionist of Basra. Many miracles and famous prayers are attributed to him. (*Mashahīr*, 88; Abu Nuᶜaym, II.198-212; *Kashif*, 111.132.)

RĀBIᶜA AL-ᶜADAWĪYA, bint Ismā'īl (d. 185 [801/2]) The most famous woman Sufi. It is said that she was stolen as a child and sold into slavery, but was released on account of her piety. She lived for a time in the desert, where she was fed miraculously by God. She later moved to Basra, where she taught Sufyān al-Thawrī and Shaqīq al-Balkhī, emphasising the importance of divine love. She left a number of fine prayers. (M. Smith, *Rābiʿa the Mystic and her Fellow-Saints in Islam.*)

SAʿĪD IBN JUBAYR, Abū ʿAbd Allāh (or Abū Muḥammad) ibn Hisham al-Asadl (d. 96 [7I3/4]) A disciple noted for his piety and learning in exegesis, tradition and fiqh. He was killed by al-Ḥujjūj ibn Yusūf. (Ibn Khallikan, I. 564—7; Nawawī, *Tahdhīb*, 278-79)

SAʿĪD IBN MUʿĀDH A contemporary of Saʿīd Ibn Zurara.

SAʿĪD IBN ZURARA A contemporary of Saʿīd Ibn Muʿadh.

SAHL AL-TUSTARĪ (203/818-283/896) Sunni theologian and mystic, his "thousand sayings" gave rise to a theological school emphasizing inward practice of the rites of worship. His analysis of the voluntary act remains classic. (SEI 488-9 [L. Massignon].)

SUFYĀN AL-THAWRĪ, Abū ʿAbd Allāh ibn Saʿīd ibn Masrūq al-Kūfī (d. 161 [777/8]) A celebrated traditionist, theologian, and ascetic. He founded an independent *madhhab*, but it did not last long. He was one of those pious men who showed their dislike of the new Umayyad regime by refusing offices in government service. (EI2, 9.770-72 [H. P. Raddatz]; GAS, I.5I8-19.)

SUHAYB ibn Sinan, "al-Rumī" (d. c. 38 [658/9]) An Arab from the Mosul region captured and enslaved as a child by Byzantine raiders. He was brought up in the Byzantine empire, and then taken to Mecca and sold. Here he joined the new Muslim community at the house of al-Arqam, and was persecuted for his faith until he made the Emigration to Medina . (Safadī, XVI. 335-8; *Isaba*, II. I88-9; Abu Nuᶜaym, I.151-6.)

TAWUS [IBN KAYSAN AL-HAWLANI] Transmitter of *aḥādīth*.

ᶜUKĀSHA (or ᶜUKKĀSHA) ibn Miḥṣan al-Asadī (d. 12 [633]) An early convert who fought at Badr. He was killed in the *ridda* wars during the caliphate of Abū Bakr. (*Isaba*, 11. 487-8; Abu Nuᶜaym, II.12-13; *Mashahīr*, 16.)

ᶜUMAR ibn al-Khaṭṭāb (d. 23 [644]) Thc second Caliph. One of the greatest figures of the early days of Islam and the founder of the Arab Empire. (SEI, 600-I [G. Levi della Vida].)

USĀMA IBN ZAYD ibn Ḥāritha (d. 54 [673/4]) Described by the Prophet as the most beloved of his Companions, he was set in charge of an expedition to Syria, preparations for which began during the Prophet's final illness. He later moved to Damascus. (*Mashahīr*, II; *Kashif*, 1. 57; *Isaba*, 1. 46.)

UWAYS AL-QARANĪ, ibn ᶜĀmir al-Murādī (d. 37?[657?]) A Yemeni, who although he never met the Prophet, was mentioned and praised by him, and was promised that he would exercise a special intercession for the believers on the Day of Judgement. Safadī tells us that 'most of his discourses concern the remembrance of death'. (Safadī, IX.456-7; Abu Nuᶜaym, n. 79-87; *Mashahīr*, 100; Ibn Marthad, 71-4.)

WUHAYB ibn al-Ward al-Makkī (d. c 153 [770/1]) A *ḥadīth* scholar who spent his life in mortification and worship, and to whom a number of miracles are attributed. He taught Ibn ʿUyayna and Ibn al-Mubārak, and a few *aḥādīth* are given on his authority by Muslim and al-Tirmidhī. (Abū Nuʿaym, V111.140-62; *Mashahīr*, 148; Massignon, *Essay*, 115; *Kashif*, 111.216.)

YAḤYĀ IBN MUʿĀDH al-Rāzi (d. 258 [871/2]) A Sufi who taught in Central Asia. One of the first to teach Sufism in mosques, he left a number of books and sayings. Despite the emphasis he placed on *rajā'*, the hope for Paradise and for God's forgiveness, he was renowned for his perseverence in worship and his great scrupulousness in matters of religion. (Abu Nuʿaym, X. 5I-70; Sulamī, 98-104; *Fihrist*, 184; GAS, 1. 644; Hujwīrī, 122-3; Massignon, *Essay*, 180-83.)

ZAYD IBN THĀBIT al-Khazrajī (d. 45 [665/6]) A Companion who joined Islam at the age of eleven. He was one of the Prophet's personal secretaries who sometimes wrote down the verses of the Qur'an as these were revealed. Participated in the official groups, appointed by Abū Bakr, ʿUmar, and ʿUthman, responsible for collecting and standardizing the written Qur'an. (*Isaba*, I. 543-4; *Mashahīr* 10.)

BIBLIOGRAPHY

Abu Nuᶜaym al-Isfahānī. *Hilyat al-awliyā wa-tabaqāt al-asfiyā* Cairo, 1351-57/1932-38.

Aḥmad b. Ḥanbal—see Ibn Ḥanbal.

ᶜAlī al-Qārī = Nūr ad-dīn ᶜAlī b. Muḥammad al-mashūr bi-Mulla ᶜAlī al-Qārī. *Al-masnū' fī maᶜrifat al-hadīth al-mawdū'*, *wa-huwa Al-Mawdūᶜāt as-sugrā.* 2nd. ed. Beirut 1389/1969.

Ansārī, Zakarīyā. *Sharh ar-Risāla al-Qushayrīya.* Published in al'ᶜArūsī, *Natāᶜij al-afkāal-qudsiyya fī bayān maᶜānī Sharh ar-Risāla al-Qushayrīyya.* Bulaq, 1290.

Aquinas, Thomas. *Summa Theologiae.* (English translation: London/New York 1964-)

Burrell, David. *Freedom and Creation in Three Traditions.* Notre Dame IN (USA), 1993.

———. *Knowing the Unknowable God.* Notre Dame IN (USA), 1986.

———. "Why not Pursue the Metaphor of Artisan and View God's Knowledge as Practical?," in Lenn E. Goodman, ed., *Neoplatonism and Jewish Thought.* Albany, 1992.

Chittick, William. *Faith and Practice in Islam.* Albany, 1992.

Dermenghem, E. *Vie des saints musulmans.* (Edition définitive). Paris, 1983.

Dhahabī, Muhammad b. Ahmad, al-. *Siyar aᶜlam al-nubalā'*. Ed. S. al-Arnā'ūt *et al.* Beirut, 1401- AH.

Fitzgerald, L. P. *Creation in al-Tafsīr al-Kabīr of Fakhr ad-Din al-Rāzī* (Ph.D. dissertation, Australian National University, 1992.)

Frank, Richard. *Al-Ghazālī and the Ashᶜarite School* Durham/London, 1994.

———. *Creation and the Cosmic System: Al-Ghazālī & Avicenna* Heidelberg, 1992.

———. "The Autonomy of the Human Agent in the Teaching of ᶜAbd al Jabbar," *Le Muséon*95 (1982) 323-55.

———. "Moral Obligation in Classical Muslim Theology," *Journal of Religious Ethics* 11 (1983) 204-23.

———. Review of Daniel Gimaret, *Théories de l'acte*, *Biblioteche Orientalis* 39 (1982) 705-15.

Freytag, G. W. *Arabum Proverbia.* Photo-reproduction of 1838-43 edition. Osnabrück, 1968.

Ghazālī, Abū Hāmid Muhammad b. Muhammad, al-. *Iḥyā' ᶜUlūm al-Dīn.* 2nd. ed. Beirut, 1979.

———. *Al-Ghazālī on the Nintey-Nine Beautiful Names of God.* (Translation of *al-Maqsād* by David Burrell and Nazih Daher. Cambridge, 1992).

———. *Tahāfut al-falāsifā*, translated by Michael Marmura (Provo UT: Brigham Young University Press, 2000).

———. *El Justo Medio en la créencia.* (Spanish translation of *al-Iqtisād fi' l-iᶜtiqād.*) Madrid, 1929.

———. *Freeedom and Fulfillment.* (English translation of *al-Munqidh* by Richard McCarthy.) Boston 1980; Fons Vitae, Louisville, KY 2000.

———. *al-Iqtisād fi' l-iᶜtiqād.* Ed. M. Abu'l-ᶜAlā. Cairo, 1972.

———. *Livre de l'amour* (French translation of *Kitāb al-ḥubb* [36] of the *Iḥyā'* by Marie-Louise Siauve.) Paris, 1986,

———. *al-Maqsād al-asnā fi sharh asmā' Allah al-husnā.* Ed. F.A. Shehadi. Beirut, 1982.

———. *Mishkāt al-anwār*, ed. A. al-ᶜAfīfī. Cairo, 1383/ 1964.

———. *Muhammad al-Gazzali's Lehre von den Stufen zur Gottesleibe*. (German transl. and introd. of Books 31-36 of the *Iḥyā'*.) Weisbaden, 1984.

———. *al-Munqidh min al-dalāl wa' l-mūsil ilā dhi' l-ᶜizza wa' l-jalāl*. Ed. and trans. Farid Jabré. Beirut, 1959).

———. *Tahāfūt al-falāsifā*. Ed. M. Bouyges. Beirut, 1927.

———. *Vivification des sciences de la foi*: Analyse et Index [of *Ihyā'*] par G.-H. Bousquet. Paris, 1955.

Gimaret, Daniel. *Théories de l'acte humain en théologie musulmane*. Paris, 1980.

———. *Les noms divins en Islam*. Paris, 1988.

———. *La doctrine d' al-Ash' arī*. Paris, 1990.

Ibn ᶜAbd al-Barr, Yūsuf. *al-Inbah ᶜalā qabā' il al-ruwā*. Ed. I. al-Aiyārī. Beirut, 1405/1985.

Ibn Hajar al-ᶜAsqalānī. *al-Isāba fī tamyīz al-Sahāba*. Cairo, 1358-9 AH.

Ibn Hanbal, Ahmad b. Muhammad. *al-Musnad*, Ed. Halabī. Cairo, 1313.

———. *Kitāb al-Zuhd*. Beirut, 1403/1983.

Ibn Hibbān, Muhammad, al-Bustī. Ed. M. Fleischhammer. Cairo, 1959.

Ibn Isḥaq. *Sīrat Rasūl Allah*, translated by A. Guillaume: *The Life of Muhammad*. Oxford, 1955.

Ibn al-Jawzī, Abü'Faraj ᶜAbd ar-Rahmān. *Al-wafā bi-ahwāl al-Mustafā*. Cairo, 1386/1966.

Ibn Māja al-Qazwīnī. *Kitāb as-Sunan*. Cairo, 1372-3/1952-3.

Ibn Marthad, ᶜAlqama. *Zuhd al-thamāniyya min al-Tābiᶜīn*. Ed. A. A. al-Faryawā'ī. Medina, 1404 AH.

Ibn al-Nadīm, Muhammad. *al-Fihrist*. Ed. G. Flügel. Leipzig, 1871-2.

ᶜIrāqī, Zayn ad-dīn Abū'l-Fadl ᶜAbd ar-Rahmān b. al-Huusayn. *Al-mugnī ᶜan haml alasfār fī' l-asfār fī tahrīj mā fī' l-Ihyā' min al-ahkbār*. At bottom of text: *Ihyā' Ulūm ad-Dīn* Cairo, 1358/1939.

Makkī, Abū Ṭālib. *Qūt al-qulūb*. Vols. 1-2: Cairo, 1310; Vols. 1-4 : Cairo 1351/1932.

Massignon, L. *Essai sur les origines du lexique technique de la mystique musulmane*. 2nd. ed. Paris, 1954. (English translation: *Essay on the Origins of the Technical Language of Islamic Mysticism*. Notre Dame IN, 1996.)

———. *The Passion of al-Hallāj. Mystic and Martyr of Islam*. Translated by Herbert Mason. Princeton, 1982.

Maydānī, Abu'l-Faḍl Aḥmad b. Muḥammad an-Naysābūrī. *Majmaᶜ al-amtāl*. Cairo 1379/1959; Beirut, 1961-2.

Munāwī, ᶜAbd ar-Raᶜūf. *Fayd al-qadīr*. (*Sharh al-Jāmi' as-saghīr*, by Suyūtī.) Cairo, 1356-7/1938.

———. *al-Ithāfat as-sanīyya bi' l-ahādīth al-qudsiyya*. ed. Muhammad ᶜAfīf az-ziᶜbī. Beirut, n.d.

Nawawi, Muhyi'l-Dīn Y̱ahyā, al-. *Tahdhīb al-asmā' wa' l-lughāt*. Cairo, 1365 AH.

Nicholson, R. A. *The Kashf al-mahjūb, the oldest Persion treatise on Sufism*. Leiden and London, 1911. (Tr. with introd. of the *Kashf al-Mahjūb* of al-Hujwīrī.)

Ormsby, Eric. *Theodicy in Islamic Thought*. Princeton, 1984.

———. "Creation and Time in Islamic Thought with Special Reference to al-G͟hazālī," in *God and Creation*, ed. David Burrell and Bernard McGinn. Notre Dame IN 1990.

Qushayrī, Abu'l-Qāsim, al-. *al-Risāla f ᶜilm al-tasawwuf*. Ed. A. Mahmūd and M. Sharīf. Cairo, 1385/1966; Cairo, 1988.

Safadī, Salāh al-Dīn Khalīl b. Aybak, al-. *al-Wāfī bi'l-wafayāt*. Ed. H. Ritter *et al.* Weisbaden, 1962-.

Sahl b. ᶜAbdullāh at-Turtarī, Abu Muhammad. *Kalām Sahl*. Collected works of Sahl: Hs. Köprülü 727.

Schimmel, Annemarie. *Mystical Dimensions of Islam*. Chapel Hill NC (USA), 1975.

Schwartz, M. "'Acquisition' [*kasb*] in Early Kalām," in S.M. Stern and A. Hourani, eds, *Islamic Philosophy and the Classical Tradition*. Columbia SC (USA), 1972.

Siauve, M,-L. *L'amour de Dieu chez Gazālī*. Paris, 1986.

———. *Livre de l'amour* (Paris: Vrin, 1986)—translation of *Kitāb al-ḥubb* of the *Iḥyā' ulūm al-dīn*

Smith, M. *Rabiᶜa the Mystic and Her Fellow-Saints in Islam*. Cambridge, 1928.

Sulamī, Abū ᶜAbd al-Rahmān, al-. *Tabaqāt al-Sufīya*. Ed. J. Pedersen. Leiden, 1960.

Watt, W. Montgomery. *Muhammad: Prophet and Statesman*. Oxford, 1961.

Wensinck, A. J. *et al. Concordance et indices de la tradition musulmane*. Leiden, 1936-69.